INSIDE
THE
ALASKA
PIPELINE

Ed McGrath

CELESTIAL ARTS
Millbrae, California

To Lynne, who helped me through some hard times.

Copyright   1977 by Ed McGrath

CELESTIAL ARTS
231 Adrian Road
Millbrae, California 94030

First Printing, April 1977
Made in the United States of America

- **Library of Congress Cataloging in Publication Data**

McGrath, Ed, 1950-
    Inside the Alaska pipeline.

    1. Alaska pipeline. I. Title.
TN879.5.M27   333.8'2   76-53336
ISBN 0-89087-138-8

1 2 3 4 5 6 7 – 82 81 80 79 78 77

Contents

Preface

From the time I started working on the pipeline, I intended to write a book about it. There hasn't been much written about the pipeline, and much of what has been written would be laughed at by someone who knew what was going on. *Playboy, Oui,* and the *L.A. Times* all sent their reporters to Alaska for a few days. They visited a few camps, hung out in bars for a couple of days, checked out the hookers, and then flew back home to crank out the most sensational story they could manage. *Rolling Stone* did a better article than anyone else, but it was still the story of an outsider looking in for a short period and then going home to write.

On the other hand, I was right in the middle of it. From the very beginning I took my typewriter to camp and wrote a page or so each day after work, made notes, and talked with fellow workers and friends about what a book on the pipeline ought to say. It was difficult to decide just how to write this book; I thought at various times of making it a

novel, or a diary, or a journalistic report with colorful anec-
dotes about pipeliners. I considered making it a book
primarily about ecology, or the effects of growth on Alaska,
or a sort of social study on living in a pipeline camp.

It was a friend of mine named Michael who set me
straight. "Ed, you ought to write a book about what you
know and what you've seen. You don't have to pretend
you're some damned journalist trying to come to terms with
the pipeline; you've been there. Just sit down and write
about it, tell what it's all about . . . You built that fucker,
man. Tell about it."

I am a member of the Laborers' International Union,
Fairbanks Local #942, and I have lived in the North pretty
steadily since 1970. I like the North, and I liked it a lot
more before the pipeline came along. I've done all the
things that one normally does if he's young and lives in the
North—built a log cabin, rafted down the Yukon River,
been awakened at five in the morning by a bear peering in
my window; and then, in 1974, I went to work on the
pipeline. In a dozen different camps, for half a dozen different companies, up and down the line, I put in my ten hours
a day, in the winter at fifty below and in the summer fighting
mosquitoes all day long. I became a pipeliner. I learned
how to rig up a piece of pipe for a sideboom to carry off, I
learned to replace broken cables on link-belt draglines, I
already knew how to handle a shovel but I became more
proficient in the use of the idiot stick than I ever cared to
be.

I sat in the warm-up shacks through the interminable
"weather days" in Prudhoe Bay, days when it was thirty
below and the wind was drifting fine snow so thick that a
man could easily get lost when he went out to take a piss.
On days like that we got down to some serious pipeline
building. The professional pipeliners love to talk, and when
they're not talking about women they're talking about
pipelines. I took notes. Sometimes I thought it was going to

drive me batty, sitting in that damn warm-up shack and listening to the inane, drunken chatter going on all around me.

An old Fairbanks ironworker friend came to my rescue. "Ed, it is my belief that there is no one in the world who doesn't know something about something. Instead of being bored and fearing for your sanity when you're on the job, you can learn. If you give these guys a chance they'll talk all day long about pussy and politics and other things they know nothing about, but the secret is to find out what they know, find out what they can do, find out where they've been and what adventures they've had, and get them to tell you about it. You wouldn't believe the things I've learned in my forty years in the construction business. You name a topic and I've learned something interesting about it from a fellow worker. They're not dummies by any means, you've just got to give them a push in the right direction to keep them from acting like they are."

I took the old timer's advice and began to learn things. The fellows I was working with had built pipelines in most of the states and in several foreign countries to boot. They had been in Iran and Venezuela and Scotland and the Netherlands, built the pipelines, collected their paychecks, and had come home looking for another one to build. They knew their pipelines, knew every phase of the business of building them, knew the equipment and the myths and stories that every pipeliner has to know to get him through the long miserable days of pipeline building. I drove people crazy, trying to get them to tell me more stories and more details about the intricate processes of welding pipe or X-raying the welds. After a few hundred hours of talking I got to like some of the cantankerous sons-of-bitches.

Just because I got to like the pipeliners is no reason to assume that I got to like the pipeline. I didn't. I was dead against its being built when I first heard about it in 1970, and if everyone were to pack up and leave tomorrow I couldn't be happier. So far as I am concerned the Alaska pipeline is just one more ripoff of the American public by the oil companies. It fits right in with the manufactured energy crisis and the constantly increasing prices of petroleum products. The only reason that this pipeline is being built is so that "Big Oil" can make money. There is enough oil in Prudhoe Bay to supply the United States for only two or three years (figuring total usage), and the building of the pipeline alone will cost about $7 billion, up considerably from the original guess of $800 million, which has proven to be barely enough to cover snow removal. And there's no guarantee that the total cost won't be ten billion by the time it's finished, though Alyeska, the consortium of oil companies responsible for the job, would surely deny this.

The American public is paying for the pipeline. That money is being thrown in the snow, pissed on, dumped in the ocean, hauled to sanitary land fills, and mysteriously disappearing into unaccountable pockets. By the time this oil hits the American market (if it ever does—a good part of it may actually be sold to Japan) it's going to be so expensive that only those who worked on the pipeline will be able to afford it.

My position is clear enough: I wish they'd pack the fucking thing up and take it back to Texas. It never needed to be built in the first place; if $7 billion were put into solar and wind energy research and development we'd be well on our way to a real solution to the energy problem. And no matter how careful the oil companies have been, they have not avoided serious environmental damage to the swamps, rivers, lakes, mountains, and plains of Alaska. In addition, the environmental damage that has been done to the cities and lifestyles of Alaskans is truly staggering. Fairbanks is short of everything but people—there are about twice as many as can comfortably fit there. There is not enough water, not enough electricity, not enough fuel, too few houses, too few streets. But Fairbanks has gained from the pipeline as well—overabundant growth, crime, pollution—all the problems of a big city. And while many Alaskans have made money on the pipeline, those who were not able to cash in on the big bucks have seen Alaska become so expensive that they can no longer afford to live there.

But with all the objections I have to the pipeline, I have to admit that it is an amazing thing. When it comes to sheer magnitude, sheer power and technology, the thing is impressive. It is so big that it almost cannot be comprehended. In terms of money spent and workers employed, it is the biggest project ever undertaken by the private sector. The line itself consists of eight hundred miles of four-foot diameter pipe, and every foot of this pipe will hold about fifty gallons of oil. The storage tanks at Valdez will hold about 60 million gallons. The tankers which will carry the oil to the lower 48 can be thought of in terms of football fields placed end to end—the longest being 350 yards and the shortest 250 yards. The main valves on the line are as tall as three-story buildings.

The list of magnitudes goes on and on. The camp kitchens turn out forty to fifty thousand meals a day. There are at any given time as many as twenty thousand people working on the line. The size of the pipe and the machines that handle it are equally amazing. Each forty-foot section of pipe weighs in at six thousand pounds. The sideboom Caterpillars that lift the pipe into place weigh over a hundred thousand pounds. Oil that is pumped into the line at Prudhoe Bay will take eight days to reach Valdez.

The pipeline is truly a remarkable thing, a tribute to the power of American techonology. If there are many questionable aspects to it, there is at least no denying its size. In fact, before the last barrel of crude is pumped out of the ground at Prudhoe Bay, the pipeline may generally be recognized as the biggest foul-up, the biggest waste of money, and the biggest rip-off of the American consumer yet perpetrated.

I am writing about the pipeline as a laborer who worked on it, and not as a journalist. Since I have done very little of the sort of research that journalists do, anyone who cares to look may find errors in this book. It could easily be the case that I say something happened in 1973 when it actually happened in 1972, or vice versa. If you're interested in exact dates, exact figures, engineering specifications, or precise data, I recommend that you have a look at something like *Time* magazine, which is always very careful to get the facts down cold. So far as I'm concerned, it's relatively unimportant whether the pipeline is 798 or 802 miles long, and I don't actually know the exact measurement. But there are things that I know very surely and which a journalist would be hardpressed to find out: what it's like to put in ten hours a day in a camp a hundred miles north of the Arctic Circle; what it feels like to go for months seeing the sun only a couple of hours a day, and what happens when a few thousand hippie laborers meet up with a few thousand redneck pipeliners. This is a book about working on the pipeline, digging the ditches, laying the pipe, smoking a little dope and kicking back in the afternoon, being horny as a goose and trying to decide whether to quit immediately or wait another week, fighting with foremen, and wishing you were home instead of getting fucked over and feeling down and out in Prudhoe Bay.

I have routinely provided pseudonyms for any individuals appearing in this book, and in one case I changed the name of a company. The last thing I would want to do is to provide my friends with cause for embarrassment or legal hassle.

Ed McGrath
College, Alaska

A Short History of the Pipeline

Although this is a short history of the pipeline, the history of the pipeline is not short by any means. As a matter of fact, it is a long, winding, mind-boggling tale of late night meetings between power brokers, multimillion dollar environmental suits, and Alaskan natives suddenly saying publicly what they had known all along—that Alaska was theirs, it had never been purchased from them or given away by them. At the heart of the story is incredible greed. It is a story of corporate oil junkies who made the Alaska connection and would not be stopped from mainlining their new greasy gold.

If this were any old pipeline it would be no more than an academic exercise to write a history of it. But the Alaska pipeline is unique because it is being built in Alaska, a place which is unquestionably and immeasurably different from any other locale in the United States. In order to come to an understanding of the pipeline it is necessary to have a look at pre-pipeline Alaska.

1

In 1960 there were about 13,000 people living in Fairbanks, and a few thousand more in the outlying areas, known as "the bush." Most of them were broke. Some were doing all right, and some were even living in high style. There has always been good money for some in Alaska, but most of them were flat broke with no prospects. They had no money because it was a pain in the ass to get a job, and the job probably wouldn't pay very much if there was one to be had, and it seemed a lot more sensible to stay at home and make do with what you had than to go out and try to make money.

Being flat broke and making do is a time-honored tradition in Alaska, and especially in 1960 it made a lot of sense. Living in Alaska has always been expensive, but only if you operated within the economy. And there have always been a lot of people around who didn't do that. They lived in cabins that they built themselves out of logs that were free for the cutting, and heat was free because logs were free, and it doesn't cost much to keep an old truck running if you only use it every now and then. In 1960 you could count on getting a moose, or a few caribou, and there was always plenty of fish for everybody, dogs and people alike. A little money could always be picked up at odd jobs to pay for gasoline and sugar and other things that couldn't be had free or in exchange for labor, and there were a lot of people who liked it that way. Some still like it that way but each year it gets harder to survive outside the economy.

Before Russians and Englishmen and Swedes came to Alaska there were not many people living there, although Alaska is a huge place, a little over 585,000 square miles, or approximately one sixth of the total U.S. area. Little groups of native Eskimos and Indians lived in small villages or simply followed the caribou as they migrated thousands of miles across the country. There was no chance for huge concentrations of people to develop—food was too hard to come by, and the living was too harsh. People froze to death and starved. If we are to believe the early writers who made the acquaintance of the natives, they all lived hard, sometimes miserable, if relatively fulfilling and satisfying lives.

It is hard to generalize about Alaska because it is so big. The Arctic coast gets about three inches of precipitation a year. The southeastern coastal forests get about three hundred. In some places there are fifty feet of snow during the winter; in others there are eighteen inches. The weather varies greatly, and so does the terrain. Besides having the highest mountains in North America, Alaska has hundreds of square miles of muskeg or swamp, flat tundra, huge powerful rivers, a tremendous amount of coastline, and forests. Most of Alaska is forested, though as you go further north, the trees get smaller and smaller. In the area around Prudhoe Bay, on the northern coast, they may be only a few inches high, though they are a hundred years old.

If there is one word that people generally associate with Alaska, it is "cold." In the winter, throughout most of the state, it is cold. But in December, January, and February, that single word is the barest beginning of a description. Goddamn is it cold! It is far colder than most people in the United States can imagine, even if they live in Minnesota and have seen forty below. Imagine a month where it *averages* forty below zero (as has happened more than once) and you begin to get an idea how cold it really is. The record temperature is minus eighty-two degrees. Even if you know about forty below, you don't know much about sixty below. At that temperature, exposed flesh freezes in about two minutes, and if that flesh happened to be wet, it would freeze instantly.

Of course, it isn't always that cold. The average January temperature in Fairbanks, which sits near the 64th parallel, about one hundred and fifty miles below the Arctic Circle, is minus seventeen degrees. During the month there are almost invariably some days that fall to sixty below or lower and some warmer days. January often sees days when the mercury climbs above the freezing mark, though not nearly enough of them. December and February average minus eleven degrees.

Contrary to popular notions, interior Alaska enjoys about five months of very pleasant weather each year. Spring, summer, and autumn can be really beautiful throughout Alaska, with temperatures getting regularly into the sixties and seventies and less often into the eighties and nineties. The ground is usually clear of snow from the first of May until the middle or end of September, and in the interior, that is, the non-coastal regions of Alaska, including Fairbanks and most of the Yukon River Valley, the average snowfall is less than three feet. Most of this is dry powder.

As you go further north the weather gets nastier. Prudhoe Bay, at the head of the pipeline, does not get the extremely cold temperatures which characterize the Yukon River Valley, but it is consistently colder and almost always windy. Summer is of shorter duration and temperatures can drop below freezing at any time. Not a good place to try to grow a garden.

It is very dry in northern Alaska, although there is water everywhere. Lakes, rivers, swamps (called muskeg in the North) and the attendant mosquitoes are everywhere, all owing to permafrost, the permanently frozen soil, rich with ice, that lies just below the surface. This serves to keep the water on the surface instead of letting it drain underground, and so an area which has about as much precipitation as Arizona claims more lakes than Minnesota.

When the idea of building a pipeline through the Alaska wilderness first reared its ugly head, all the facts I have just mentioned were well known. Oil exploration had been going on since the late fifties, and thousands of men had worked on the drilling and seismological crews which found the oil. But although permafrost was within the oil companies' realm of knowledge, they had no real understanding of it, and certainly no respect for it. In 1968 Atlantic-Richfield (ARCO) hit gold—an estimated oil reserve of 9.6 billion barrels in Prudhoe Bay. It didn't take long to start the wheels moving.

In June of 1969 three oil companies, ARCO, British Petroleum, and Humble Oil, applied for a permit to build an eight-hundred-mile pipeline from Prudhoe Bay to Valdez, an ice-free port on the southern coast of Alaska. These three oil companies had put together a company which was known as TAPS—Trans Alaska Pipeline System. But the permit which they applied for was an afterthought. They had already bought what they considered the essentials for a pipeline: eight hundred miles of forty-eight-inch-diameter pipe and many truckloads of parkas for the men who would build the pipeline. The pipe came from Japan and the parkas from Taiwan. American producers could have manufactured the pipe, but TAPS was in a godawful hurry; there would be no waiting around for an American plant to gear up for producing four-foot-diameter pipe. The three Japanese companies came through: In the fall of 1969 the pipe began to arrive at Valdez, Fairbanks, and Prudhoe Bay, where it sat in piles and rusted until 1975.

Although TAPS had eight hundred miles of pipe and enough parkas for everyone, they had absolutely no idea about how to build a pipeline across Alaska. With all the greed and short-sightedness of oil junkies, they wanted to get their hands on the Prudhoe Bay oil. Never mind that this pipeline was to be built in a place where the temperature fluctuates from sixty degrees below to a hundred above. Never mind that the ground they would be building on owes its existence to its frozen state, and when thawed turns into a bottomless quagmire. To hell with the fact that Alaskan communications, transportation and technology in general was for the most part at the log cabin, kerosene lamp, and dog sled stage. TAPS went ahead and announced that it was going to flat build itself a pipeline, that it would cost $800 million, would solve U.S. energy problems, and would be done pretty soon.

They were not only going to build a pipeline, but they were going to build it exactly as if it were located in Texas. Just weld it together, bury it, and forget it. Someone pointed out to them that if they buried it in permafrost the 160 degree oil coursing through the line would thaw out the ground that the pipe was resting on, thus virtually assuring that the pipe would break as it sagged. TAPS hired some experts to fly over the proposed route of the line, and when the plane landed they had it all figured out: they would put forty-five miles of the line above ground; that would take care of the permafrost problem. The fact that there were over four hundred miles of permafrost to be traversed wasn't taken into account or, more likely, TAPS didn't even know it existed. In the fall of 1975 the engineers were still changing their minds about where the pipe should be above ground and where below.

The first fiasco came early, in 1969. The well-known "conservationist" Walter J. Hickel was then governor of Alaska, and he thought that it was imperative to have a road built to Prudhoe Bay. The truckers didn't like the fact that all supplies needed on the North Slope were being flown in, and Wally Hickel, who owns two snazzy hotels in Alaska, was a man who stood for moderate progress, or progressive moderation, or some such combination. Now, this wasn't the first road that was built to the North Slope. Previously there had been winter roads, made by heaping up snow, then flattening and packing down the surface. To be sure, this kind of road disappears every spring. Hickel's boys decided to build a permanent road. They scraped the moss off the tundra and thus provided a smooth surface for trucks to run on. Unfortunately, spring came in 1969, as it always does, and the frozen ground, which no longer had any moss to insulate it and keep it frozen, thawed. The famous "conservationist" had produced a four-hundred-mile ditch full of oozing mud. The damage has not been repaired and may never be.

The oil companies and their contractors knew how to build pipelines, but they knew almost nothing about permafrost or cold weather or how hard it is to get anything done at sixty below, when machines won't run and people don't want to. Time and time again they have shown that they simply don't know enough about the environment they are working in. When seventy thousand gallons of fuel were spilled on the tundra in early 1976, it was because someone had forgotten that he wasn't in Texas, but Alaska. As the temperature rose sixty degrees in twelve hours, not an uncommon occurrence, the fuel in the tank expanded, broke a valve, and poured onto the tundra.

In 1970 eight hundred miles of pipe were stacked in yards beside the road and the oil junkies were crying that they wanted to start laying pipe. They claimed that only two things were holding them up—the natives and the environmentalists. In reality there were three reasons for not beginning. In addition to the first two, the oil companies still had no idea how to build a pipeline in Alaska. Since the third reason for not building the line existed, the first two were actually to the advantage of the oil companies.

The ownership of most of the land in Alaska was in question when TAPS applied for its permit to build the pipeline. They needed an eight-hundred-mile long, one-hundred-foot wide swath across the length of Alaska, and it was not clear just who could sell or lease them this swath. The Alaskan natives were dead set against the pipeline coming near their villages and crossing their hunting and fishing grounds. On the one hand there was the fear that the waters would be polluted and the game spooked, and on the other the matter of ownership. One thing was clear—when white people came to Alaska, they had simply moved in. They had bought no land, and the natives damn sure hadn't given them any. There was the usual fuzzy history of treaties and promises. The natives were at this very time in the process of bargaining both for money and for land to call their own, and before the pipeline builders could be issued a permit, the native land claims had to be settled.

And then there were the environmentalists. The Wilderness Society, the Environmental Defense Fund, and the Friends of the Earth sought and obtained a court injunction against pipeline construction. These groups pointed out a few obvious facts about permafrost and cold weather and the fight was on. In large part they won their fight, although the pipeline finally was built. If it had not been for the environmentalist groups, the pipeline would have unquestionably been a total fiasco, a five-mile wide, eight-hundred-mile long ditch full not of mud, but of oil. If the oil companies had gone ahead and built their line as first planned, it is doubtful that any oil would have reached Valdez at all. That is still in doubt, but thanks to the efforts of the environmentalists, less so.

In 1970 Alyeska Pipeline Service Company, Inc., came into the picture. TAPS by this time had proven itself totally inefficient, a bumbling bunch of oil-crazed junkies or, in the terminology of a pipeliner, a group with its head up its corporate ass. Nothing was happening. Besides owning eight hundred miles of rusting pipe, which was costing several million dollars a year to store, and a large number of inferior parkas, the pipeline was simply not moving. Alyeska was a consortium of the original oil companies, British Petroleum, ARCO, and Humble, which was owned by Standard of New Jersey, now Exxon, and some new ones—Standard Oil of Ohio, which merged with BP, and some others. I was never able to follow Alyeska through its various reorganizations and permutations, but there were many of them, with new companies joining up, others cutting their percentages, mergers, financings, and refinancings.

At any rate, Alyeska started to do what they have always done best—public relations. Slick is not the word for it. In 1971 the whole world learned that Alyeska was a bunch of the nicest guys that one could ever wish to meet, and that they were just trying to bring some oil south so folks could heat their homes and drive their cars. The world also learned in 1971 that if Alyeska didn't get the pipeline built everyone would suffer and we'd be in hock to the Arabs. And furthermore, Alyeska, an incredibly nice bunch of incredibly nice guys, really cared about Alaska and the down home folks there, including pesky Eskimos, and cared about permafrost and caribou and the little fishes in the streams. They put ads in all major magazines, bought T.V. time, and put together slide shows. They hired unctuous P.R. men to explain things to obnoxious crowds of college students. I saw one of these slide shows in 1972 in Boulder, Colorado, while a large group of security guards held back students who knew slick P.R. when they saw it.

But Alyeska did a good job, as they continue to do. Ten million dollars and one energy crisis later, the world was ready for the Alaska pipeline. The government of Alaska didn't need to be convinced. They were ready from the beginning to sell out to the oil companies. Alaskan construction firms, businessmen, bankers, and hookers were glad to see the pipeline coming. They were ready to go in 1969, when 1400 corporations signed up to do business in Alaska. By 1973 there had been millions of dollars worth of equipment sitting idle for four years, and the owners of that equipment were putting pressure on the federal and state governments to push the pipeline bills through. The Alaskan state government, in addition to its interest in growth and business promotion, was rapidly going broke, having spent most of the $900 million gained from the lease of the Prudhoe Bay oil fields. They wanted more. As it turned out, if they had gotten about ten times more, it might have done some good in repairing the damage caused by the pipeline. In December of 1973 the permits were issued. The natives had been given back some of the land which was theirs in the first place, and the environmentalists had settled on the best compromise they could wrangle.

There was one other momentous decision in 1973. All homesteading land was closed to the public. I was out looking over some country, stepping off a five-acre plot on land that was being offered by the state of Alaska. I came back into town to try to borrow the fifty dollars that I needed to file my claim, but found that the homesteading days were over. America had come to Alaska. From now on land was going to cost big money. People who had been living in the bush illegally—that is, on land that they didn't own—were harassed. Cabins were burned. And because there was no more cheap living available, people who had come to Alaska to homestead were now thinking about working on the pipeline. In the summer of 1973 I was not prepared to believe that the pipeline would ever be built, and even if it were built I had no intention of working on it. A lot of people were thinking that way in '73.

In 1960 there were only a small number of people living in Fairbanks and the outlying parts, and most of them were broke. The same situation existed in 1973, although the population tallied a few thousand more. Jobs were very hard to come by and generally didn't pay enough to make them worth taking, though if lucky one could work on the North Slope at $2.50 an hour for an eighty-hour week. That was big money. The unemployment rate was running about 25 percent, but that included some of the most blissfully unemployed people in the country. The correct figure for unemployment would almost certainly be higher, because there were many people who were just doing without jobs, living in the tradition of the old Alaska. For the most part the people who were coming to Alaska were not coming to look for jobs, but for a life where a job would be superfluous. Before homesteading was closed, those who chose to come to Alaska were young, idealistic, and looking for a home. They fit right in. In other parts of the country they were hippies but when they came to Alaska and learned to use an axe they were just like the people who had been doing this sort of thing for the last hundred years.

But things were changing. In January of 1974 the Laborers' Union, Local #942, held a general sign-up. They were gearing up for the pipeline. Three thousand young Fairbanksans put their names on the list to work on the pipeline. Most of these three thousand were later bumped off the lists because they failed to pay their dues, but rumor had it that there was big money just around the corner. The pipeline was coming! I didn't sign up at that time, because I still didn't want to work for the oil companies and because I had some kind of naive faith that this just couldn't happen. It was the summer of 1974 when I and many other young men went to work on the pipeline.

It had suddenly become obvious that we could be against the pipeline as much as we wanted, but there would be no massive resistance; if we didn't take the jobs others would. There were thousands of people coming to town, hungry for jobs. Alyeska had the money, and they were buying whatever they wanted; the resistance we could offer didn't amount to a pisshole in the snow.

We went to work. It was easy to get a job, especially if you were an Alaska resident. The local unions were enforcing (to some extent) the Alaska hiring policy: natives had preference, followed by other residents of Alaska. All you had to do, in essence, was to show your driver's license down at the union hall, wait a few days, and you had a job. But it was the lowest paying job on the line, even if $9.60 per hour plus room and board doesn't seem all that bad. Laboring is also the dullest job on the pipeline, and laborers are the low men on the totem pole when it comes to any on-the-job power struggle. Here again, Alyeska demonstrated its usual concern for Alaskans. Men who had all their lives run equipment in mines, men who knew how to keep a Cat running in the dead of winter, men who had grown up welding, were made laborers or "bullcooks," the camp version of a maid. Alaskans by and large are skilled people, used to doing anything that needs to be done— fixing their machinery or building houses—but they couldn't get into the appropriate unions. Further, Alaskans are used to autonomy, or being their own damn bosses, as it is more commonly put, but they were shoved into the hierarchy of the pipeline, put into laborers' positions where they would make no decisions of their own. But it was that or no job at all. The good jobs—the welding, mechanicking, truck driving, equipment operating, and especially the foremans' positions, went to outsiders, as anyone not from Alaska is called.

While Alyeska was busy convincing the world that the Alaska pipeline was a good, noble, and much needed undertaking, they were also figuring out how to build it. They had hired Bechtel, a San Francisco-based organization, and others to do the engineering and quality control. Alyeska was in essence just a bunch of executives borrowed from other corporations, and they wisely relegated themselves to the position of overseers and public relations men. All the actual work would be done by subcontractors. The pipe was sitting in stacks beside the road, and so long as no one had yet figured out how to build the pipeline, that was a good place for it. Alyeska was talking to the unions and getting an idea of what labor would cost them. The price of the pipeline climbed steadily through the years, from $800 million, to $2 billion, to $4 billion, to $5.6 billion, and finally to $7 billion. We began to learn about cost-plus contracts.

Cost-plus is a very great influence in making the pipeline what it is, i.e. one of the most wasteful projects ever undertaken. When you're working on cost-plus, you, as a contractor, perform a service for Alyeska, and any amount of money you spend to get the job done will be reimbursed, plus a percentage of that (around 10 percent, the rumor goes) as profit. In practical terms what it means is this: the more money you spend, the more money you make. The result is that if you can get away with hiring three laborers for a two-laborer job, you're making a larger profit. If you burn two thousand gallons of fuel instead of one thousand, you make more money. Any of us simple folks can see, as the saying goes, "This ain't no fucking way to build a pipeline."

The advantage of this system is that the job will almost certainly get done. Or at least it seems that way. If you have your contractors scrimping and saving and trying to cheat on materials and labor, god knows what kind of a mess you might end up with. The disadvantage of this system is that everybody and his brother-in-law is lining his pockets with it. It's too good to be true, and especially with the lack of supervision there will necessarily be when workers are spread out over eight hundred miles. Even if Alyeska wanted to control costs (and there have been only feeble indications that they want to), they probably couldn't.

And so the slogan and attitude has arisen: "Nothing too good for the pipeline." If there's any chance that some machine or material will be needed—buy it! If you think you might need a couple of extra welders—hire them! That's right, Jack, there's more money where this came from! While I worked on the pipeline, I saw not the slightest concern for efficiency or conservation of any sort. When it was a question of using more materials or using less, we invariably used more. There is an old construction dictum that goes, "If you have a one-man job, let one man do it. If you put two hands on the job, they'll probably stand around and bullshit all day and not get the job done at all." On the pipeline, the reverse of this old saying is in force. If anyone can see any reason at all for having two men on a job, there will be at least two men working on it, and probably four. And naturally they'll need a foreman.

The notable overabundance of workers on the pipeline is often attributed to "union featherbedding," but that's a matter of barking up the wrong tree. It's the cost-plus contract that is at the heart of all the waste and superfluous energy that goes into the pipeline. Somebody is making money on that waste. The unions aren't demanding that a new worker be hired when one quits a crew of six that hasn't had anything to do for weeks. The contractor is the one who makes sure that he keeps the numbers up. And the buck is sure to be passed. Pretty soon Alyeska will start crying about how their oil has to be priced higher to take care of the overrun in production costs. They'll be playing the percentage game too. And in the end, it's the people who have to put gasoline in their cars and heat their homes who'll pay for it. Oil companies don't lose money.

In actuality, Alyeska came to Alaska with nothing but money, and began spending it, convinced that they could buy the goodwill of Alaskans. Part of going to work on the pipeline is an orientation session that includes a beautiful film about Indians and Eskimos which points out that Alyeska is in sympathy with their needs and has their welfare at heart. And perhaps that is true, though we have little reason to believe it. But even given that, what Alyeska lacks is a knowledge of what the natives' needs are, and an understanding of their lifestyles and priorities. Alyeska carried out a big, well publicized public service effort to get rid of all the fifty-five-gallon oil drums that the Army left scattered all over the tundra during and after World War II. To do this they brought in a truly amazing bit of technology—a machine riding on super low-pressure treads that could crawl over the delicate tundra without damaging it or sink-ing in. They collected the steel drums, smashed them up and shipped them off.

Laudable?

Not if you happen to be an Alaskan native subsisting in a bush community. Oil drums are valuable, even if they are rusty. Natives (and other people in Alaska too—I used to have twenty or so drums in my yard) use these drums in any number of ingenious ways. You can use them for burning trash in. You can store gasoline or oil in them. You can use them for salting fish. Cut the ends out of them and weld them together and make a culvert. Make a boiler. Use them as foundation piers for a house. Make a smokehouse. Use them for flotation in rafts. Make a stove. Cut them up and use the steel for any number of things. The list goes on and on. It would have been a real public service to distribute them to the villages, or even to sell them for a reasonable price there. So the touted tundra clearing project did not win many hearts.

Nor did Alyeska have any concern for the people who live in Alaska's cities. No consideration was taken of the lifestyles and peculiarities of Alaskans. I am not here to deny that they pay good wages to those who work for them. I've never made so much money before and may never again. But there is a price tag on that money, and it isn't just ten hours of work a day. Fairbanks used to have a higher quality of life, if a lot shakier economy, than it does today. We didn't used to be much troubled with pollution or crime or traffic jams, and now we are. People didn't used to be so hungry for money or strapped for money that they'd go off to work and leave their children home alone. Now they do. There have actually been broadcast on radio, pleas from children whose parents left them alone to work on the Slope. A twelve-year-old girl is left in charge of her four-year-old brother. They are running out of food, or the plumbing is frozen up, or the furnace has stopped. Would their parents please contact them. There are thousands of children being neglected in Alaska, and all because of the inconceivable pressure to make money which is part of the new Alaska. But Alyeska hasn't put up any money for day-care centers, although they caused the problem in the first place.

The point is clear: Alyeska offers money, and lots of it. But they don't offer it to everyone, and not everyone has profited by their invasion. Those who haven't profited have been caught up in outrageous inflation and surely have been given no solace.

Although Alyeska was constantly screaming about the need to start laying their pipe, the actual pipelining comes near the end of the project. Before getting down to pipelining, there were thousands of other things that had to be accomplished. First of all, the old Hickel ditch had to be replaced with a road that trucks could drive on. Even before the permit for the pipeline was issued, construction began on the road. In pre-pipeline days, there was a road north from Fairbanks only as far as Livengood, a nearly abandoned mining town eighty miles from Fairbanks. From Livengood, the road had to go north to the Yukon River, cross it, and wind its way up and down and through the Brooks Range, cross dozens of creeks and rivers, and finally traverse the tundra between the Brooks Range and Prudhoe Bay.

Now the road is built, a ribbon of gravel heaped five feet high and requiring constant maintenance. In the spring it gets soft and muddy as the snow melts and the ground thaws out. Loads are limited to 50 percent of what they would usually be. In the summer the road is rough, full of potholes and washboard. It's also dusty—a high-balling truck leaves a quarter-mile stream behind it. When fall comes the rains and first wet snows turn the road to mud puddles again; in the winter it's icy and slick at first but becomes a good smooth road as the temperatures drop. Then the only problem is to keep the snowdrifts off it.

There were also camps to be built—twenty-three of them, with a capacity of about eighteen thousand men and women. On the southern half of the line there were already some facilities, and there was one old camp in the north. In Fairbanks, part of Ft. Wainwright was leased from the Army and turned into offices and dormitories. But for the most part contractors began to haul in trailers and jack them into position. Aside from BP's Prudhoe Bay Camp, which is made of modular structures, the rest of the living areas look like a poor compromise between Army and refugee camps. In a country that had previously felt comfortable only with log cabins, outhouses, and wood-burning stoves, there were now trailers of shiny metal and shiny plastic, sewer treatment plants, and a pervasive smell of diesel fumes. It was a new culture, instant culture, and as usual, a culture of the most tawdry kind available. America had come to Alaska.

The people of Alaska began to think about things they had never considered before. The newspapers were full of pipeline news and the bars were full of Southerners. Hookers lined the streets of the downtown areas. In some ways it began to look like another gold rush, just another boom. As Forty Mile, Dawson City, and Livengood were famous in 1898, so now everyone began to hear tales of Chandalar, Old Man, Franklin Bluffs, Isabel Pass, Valdez, and Cold Foot. Now there was no more thought of going out and building a cabin in the bush; the Alaskan thing to do was to join up with a union, get a job, and go to the Slope. There was no question but that Alyeska had won.

Going to the Slope

Fairbanks International Airport isn't as big as JFK, but has more activity per square foot. The terminal building is full. The parking lot is full. There aren't any more cars for rent, not even at twenty-five dollars a day and twenty-five cents a mile. People are lined up at every ticket counter and lined up at the baggage carousel. They're streaming off the planes from Seattle and Dallas, wearing cowboy clothes or business suits, coming either to work on the pipeline or check on some facet of it. They go straight to the Alyeska information desk and start firing questions at the three miniskirted girls who are there to answer questions. The men want to know how to find H. C. Price's office, how to find Houston Contracting's office, how to get a job on the pipeline, what the girls are doing after they get off work.

It was November and I was getting ready to go to the Slope. Not that I wanted to, by any means. I was by now a veteran of so many pipeline jobs that I'd hate to try to count

18

them all, and there was no more mystery in it for me. There was nothing I wanted more than to stay home and read by the fire, but I was broke again and figured that I'd better try to stick it out for a month and make some money. The jobs start to shut down about the middle of December and then open up again in mid-January, so it was do it now or face two more months of being flat broke.

Slope or *North Slope* is Alaska shorthand for the north slope of the Brooks Range, a majestic stretch of mountains running roughly east-west across Alaska inside the Arctic Circle. You can see them about eighty miles off, rising tall and jagged, when you look south from Prudhoe Bay on a clear day. When you go to the Slope, it means that you're going to work in one of the camps along the pipeline route, dots on the map surrounded by nothing. Actually there are a number of camps on the south slope of the Brooks Range too, but so far as Alaskans are concerned it's all North Slope.

I was, to put it as mildly as I know how, a bit cynical about the whole prospect of going to work. When I got my first job, I was ready to move mountains with a number two round-pointed shovel if anyone wanted me to. The highest paying job I'd ever had before was $4.00 an hour, and I'd worked hard for that. I was about to be paid $9.60 an hour plus benefits and room and board. I could hardly believe it! I was ready to tear ass. I'd changed my shirt and bought a new pair of gloves. Damn was I glad to have a job.

But now I was a little calmer about the whole thing. I knew that I probably wouldn't have to work very hard, and that it was highly unlikely I'd be fired even if I knew nothing at all about the job and, in fact, the worst part of the job would probably be boredom, having to put up with the bureaucrats and standing around in the cold. I figured that come what may I could handle it, and if it was too bad, I could always quit and go back to the hall for another job more to my liking.

The route to a job on the pipeline begins at the union hall—that's Laborers' Local #942 of Fairbanks, and let no slander be spoken against it! So one morning I got up and went down in time to make the 9:30 A.M. call.

Most people who live outside the construction racket—that is, those who are paying for this madness rather than cashing in on it—do not know what the inside of a labor hall looks like. If you go into a hall in Kansas City or Seattle, you will see a collection of hefty middle-aged men, slightly misshapen by years of packing buckets of concrete and cinder blocks and drinking beer, sitting around a dingy room playing cards. There are rarely any jobs to be had in these places and most of the laborers are drawing unemployment (or wishing that their benefits hadn't run out) and sitting around the hall to see what might pop up. But in Fairbanks it's a different scene.

Fairbanks laborers are predominantly young and for the most part just got into the racket. Compared to the quiet card playing of other halls, the Fairbanks scene is one of sheer chaos. On any day of the week you will see a ragtag collection of All-American stoned-out hippies, a scattering of Indians and Eskimos, and the old-timers, some of them professional laborers, others just cashing in on the pipeline. Then too, strange as it may seem, there will be a large group of Cuban exiles, eager for jobs and shouting at the dispatcher about their reputations in Miami for "making with the shovel." There are four separate union lists—A, B, C, and D—but we need only concern ourselves with the first three, since the lowly D-listers never get any jobs.

In order to get on the C list you must have one year of residence in Alaska, or fake it, or have two years of experience in the construction industry, which is even easier to fake. Anyone who can't meet either of these requirements belongs on the D list and should go back to college for a while. The laborers are without a doubt the most educated of the pipeline workers. A considerable number have college degrees, and you don't rate at all unless you got through at least one year. The professional pipeliners, on the other hand, are usually the sort who made it through the eighth grade or maybe almost got a high school diploma but got into a fight with the principal at the last moment.

I am on the A list. That means I have endured more than eight hundred hours of union work and now can claim my reward, which is a job any day of the week. My position is further enhanced by the fact that I haven't worked for the last two months and thus have a high number on the A list. When you quit a job you are placed on the bottom of the list and then your number rises as people above you are hired. I'm number 545. That means there are 544 guys ahead of me, but most of them are in Hawaii or California sitting out the winter, having made their easy money in the summertime. Today I most likely can not only get a job, but get any job I happen to cotton to.

The dispatcher calls out the jobs available in a shorthand which is incomprehensible to anyone who doesn't know the racket. The first call: "H. C. Price, Livengood, needs seven general laborers, seven tens, indefinite. You'll be working with a crusher." A chorus of "Fuck Price!" "Fuck crushers!" and "Nobody will stick at that job long!" goes up through the hall. By way of explanation, H. C. Price is the contractor responsible for building the pipeline between the Yukon River and a spot south of Fairbanks where another company takes over, and Livengood is a pipeline camp a few miles from the old mining town of Livengood, about eighty miles north of Fairbanks. "Seven tens" refers to the work week—seven days a week, ten hours a day. Everything over forty hours is, of course, time and a half, and added to this is travel time, or the time that it takes you to ride out to the worksite on a bus in the morning. You ride home at night on your own time. A crusher is a terrible series of huge machines that turn rock into gravel, and working around one is one of the dirtiest, noisiest, most disgusting jobs imaginable. I worked on a crusher for four days one time and would never consider it again. That's what is referred to as a C-list job. Those on the A list don't lower themselves.

I elbow my way toward the dispatcher's window, not paying much attention to the calls, other than to note that Green Construction needs eighteen laborers at Old Man camp, a dingy little place just seven miles this side of the Arctic Circle. That call draws frenzied shouting and clapping. Everyone knows what that means—eighteen laborers got stoned, drunk, fucked up, and told the foreman they were quitting because it was too cold. Four or five of the laborers that quit are in the hall now telling the story.

"So about lunchtime we all got together and went over to Pete and said, 'Pete, it's too cold. We want to go home.' And Pete drawls, 'All of you? Goddamn, you fellows are going to get me fired yet. But that's all right, when a man's gotta go, he's gotta go. Now what should I put down under reason for quitting?' "

" 'Too cold.' "

" 'Come on, boys, you know I can't put down something like that.' "

And so it goes. It's not even remarkable anymore. Crews are constantly shut down because half the labor force decides all at once that it's too cold and wants to go home. But it's still exciting to hear that call: "Eighteen laborers for Green at Old Man, and if you don't want to work, don't take the job."

I decide that I want the job with West Texas Contracting in Prudhoe Bay, which has put in a call for two laborers. The weather there is the nastiest of any place on the line, but the camp is nice, and I've heard good things about West Texas. It is not what you call a high-ballin' outfit. It'll be a fine job.

The dispatcher is now calling out: "Is there anybody between one and one hundred on the list?" There isn't. Some of those names have been on the list for two years.

"Anybody between one-oh-one and two hundred?" Again, no one. The people on the top of the list made their money last spring and summer and are still on vacation, or maybe settled into a frugal early retirement.

"Two-oh-one to three hundred?"

A couple of guys call out, "Here!" They want the jobs in Livengood, where they can drive into Fairbanks and party once in a while.

I get the job I want. I sign the form allowing twenty cents an hour to be deducted from my check for the union, a small price to pay. "Do you know where the West Texas office is?" asks the dispatcher.

"Sure, no problem." I've had so many jobs I think I know where everyone's office is.

After leaving the union hall with my job referral slip, I journeyed through the ice fog-bound streets to Ft. Wainwright, the Fairbanks headquarters of Alyeska. In order to work on the pipeline, you have to be in possession of a pipeline badge, a little plastic-encased card that gives your name, job, social security number, and any medical peculiarities you might have, and includes your picture. I smoked a joint on the way out and arrived in good spirits for the familiar session of waiting in line, having my picture taken, and answering the questions that are always asked. It was good to step inside Building 1004, a cinderblock job of World War II vintage which Alyeska leases from the army. My first pipeline job was with the outfit that remodeled this building. I went downstairs to the badge room and got in line.

Although one is required to turn in one's old badge when getting a new one, I have never turned one in, but rather have a whole string of them in my house. Fashioned into a mobile and hanging from my living room ceiling, they serve as a document of sorts regarding my adventures on the pipeline. I have badges from half a dozen different contractors spanning the whole northern half of the line, and in several cases more than one from a contractor. Each member of my collection shows me in some drugged state, and all in all they are a fitting document of the extremes to which the prospect of working for an oil company can drive a man.

It was in the badge room that I encountered my first Texan. Now, in order to be a Texan it is not wholly necessary to come from Texas. "Texan" is more of a generic term for any southerner who has come north to work on the pipeline, and includes a goodly number of workers from Alabama, Louisiana, Oklahoma, and the other pipelining states. They were lounging all over the badge room. "Honey," one paunchy southerner was saying to the girl taking the pictures, "if you'd like to take an extra pitcher of me to keep for yerself, yer welcome to do that. I have often been known to excite passion in women." Having made this speech he turned around and winked at me.

"Where did you learn to say that," I snarled, "from a John Wayne movie?"

He looked shocked for a moment and then drawled, "You'd best not let your mouth overload your ass, son." I had momentary visions of getting gored in the head by cowboy boots.

"Suck my dick," I said calmly.

"I would," he grinned, "if I thought you had one."

The secretary was on the phone trying to get hold of a security guard. "Don't bother," I told her, "it was a joke."

I have learned that if you intend to get along with a Louisiana welder, one way that will gain you respect is to mount a staunch attack and then tell him that it was only a joke. Some of these guys don't understand the more subtle varieties of humor, but can easily get behind an outright attack on "The Duke," if done in the right spirit.

"Shucks, I was only funnin' you," I drawled. "Where you from, good buddy?"

"Louisiana," he answered, forgetting for a moment that we were almost ready to punch it out, "and mighty proud of it."

"See," I pointed out to another longhair standing beside me, "he comes from Louisiana, just like I thought. These Louisiana boys appreciate a good joke." I started to laugh uncontrollably and knock piles of papers off the desk.

"What's got into him?" asked the pipewelder.

"Too much Jack Daniels," answered the longhair.

I had gotten signed up with West Texas Contracting, giving them my referral slip and initialling the xeroxed form whereby everyone who goes to work on the line agrees that he won't indulge in the use of alcoholic beverages or drugs not prescribed by a physician while in camp.

"I got a job!" I shouted when I came in the front door.

"Sit down and smoke some dope," commanded Ace, sitting on the living room floor wearing L.A. shades, ten pounds of weed spread out around him. Because Ace is six-feet-four and with his long blond hair and full beard looks like a Viking wearing shades, he has presence. His real name is Walter Surgeon, but since he went to medical school for a year and on one occasion became a hero by stitching up a nasty chainsaw cut with nylon fishing line and then packing the victim five miles to the nearest road, he has been known as Ace Surgeon. He also carries a full line of pharmaceutical supplies.

"Ace," I said, "you're just the man I was wanting to see. I'm going to the Slope tomorrow."

"Excellent," he said, handing me one of his professionally rolled joints. "That gives us an excuse to go out to dinner and engage in some problem drinking."

"Oh no, not me," I said. "I always go to my jobs completely wasted, but not this time. I have to be at the airport at eight tomorrow morning."

"Well, if you have to be up that early in the morning there's no point in going to bed. What do you say, I'll take you and Sylvia out to dinner."

We started with eighteen-dollar-a-crack lobster at the Switzerland, Fairbanks' poshest eating place, where Ace terrorized the waitress with constant suggestions that they "engage in some heavy petting" or "fly off to Acapulco for the weekend." Sylvia held forth with a passionate tirade against sexism while she fondled my crotch. We settled on a twenty-dollar tip as compensation for mental cruelty that Ace had inflicted on the waitress. Sylvia and I were hot to go home. Ace, however, insisted on buying us a drink at a little bar known as Chilkoot Charlies, ten miles down the road toward Anchorage. The night continued with a general tour of the bars of Fairbanks. Then we decided to cruise Second Avenue a few times to see if there were any hookers outside at forty below. There were. The night ended with a mad ride to my house in Ace's Lincoln. At this point it was absolutely inconceivable that I could pack my hardhat and work clothes, get my truck started, and drive to the airport by eight in the morning.

And to swing the balance completely, Sylvia was pouting and whining that I didn't love her anymore: I was going to take off to Prudhoe Bay for a whole month without fucking her. In truth, this was a concern to me too. I have been horny in Prudhoe Bay before, and also Livengood, Old Man, Five Mile, Prospect Creek, and a couple of other camps, and I am of the opinion that one should take every precaution to ward off that miserable possibility.

"Come to bed, babe," cooed Sylvia. "There are more important things than building pipelines."

When I woke up at four-thirty the next afternoon I had to call West Texas Contracting and tell them that I had missed the flight because my car wouldn't start, not a particularly exciting excuse but certainly good enough for any company bearing the name of West Texas Contracting. The next day I was back on the phone at ten in the morning with the same excuse. The secretary suggested I take a cab.

"Do you know how much a cab would cost!" I shouted. "Twelve fucking dollars!"

"Pipeliners make a lot of money," snapped the secretary. "Don't worry about it."

I was not in reality overly remorseful about having missed two days of work. I had taken the job at the union hall on Monday, and would have flown to Prudhoe on Tuesday and started work on Wednesday, thus getting paid for Wednesday, Thursday, and Friday at straight time and Saturday and Sunday at time and a half. But at the rate I was going I would not start work until Friday. While it would seem that this delay would cut me out of two days' pay, those two days are fairly insignificant when it comes to tabulating net pay. It is all a matter of tax brackets and getting the largest amount of money for the smallest amount of work, which, as a good union man I feel is the duty of the oppressed workers of the world. When one works a week on the pipeline he grosses somewhere around a thousand dollars, and taxes are withheld as if this poor oppressed worker were making executive wages of fifty-some thousand a year. This holds true even if our theoretical oppressed worker works only one month out of the year. He makes four thousand in the month and has two thousand withheld as taxes, and then has to involve himself in the intricacies of tax law in order to claim some small part of that expropriated two thousand as his own.

On the other hand, if one works only Friday, Saturday, and Sunday, he grosses four hundred dollars and takes home about three hundred of that—that's three hundred dollars for three days' work, as opposed to five hundred for seven days' work, surely something to shout about when one applies the old "Largest Amount of Money for the Smallest Amount of Work" law. It is further in the worker's best interest to work the weekend first because in every pipeline camp steak is served on Saturday night and prime rib on Sunday.

And now I am at the airport, in the cafeteria, sitting at a table with Ace and Sylvia, trying to keep it together for the upcoming four-hundred-mile flight to Prudhoe Bay. I am vaguely aware that Sylvia has my pants unzipped again and has ferreted her way through two layers of longjohns toward the goal she has sought constantly for the last two days. The prospect of our being separated for the next month is not a pleasant one and ever since I came home from the union hall we have been trying to get in enough fucking so that neither of us will need it for a month. At the moment my cock is so sore and red and shrivelled up that I'm sure I can make it through the next week without missing sex at all. Sylvia on the other hand is completely indefatigable and now is whispering in my ear that she is going to blow me under the table.

"I think I'd better go check and see if the flight is going to leave on time," says Ace.

Ace's departure brings up drug-fired paranoia about the prospects of missing another flight. As it is now, I have been up for the last thirty-six hours while performing approximately eight acts of normal and deviant sex, smoked untold amounts of Ace's hundred-dollar-an-ounce superweed, and gone out drinking twice. Sylvia has now slipped beneath the table and is moaning while I try to keep a straight face and drink some more Coca-Cola. I am beginning to wonder whether I'll make it to Prudhoe Bay at all.

And I am worried too about the little bag of weed that I have stuck in my left boot. There's really nothing to be concerned about; I've almost never gone to a pipeline job without my stash. It doesn't do much for your efficiency, but on the other hand you need something to get you through those boring days of sitting and waiting for parts for broken machines. It's part of working on the pipeline. A friend of mine had a job as a flagman. He stood on the road, stopping the trucks coming from one direction and letting those coming from the other direction through, and then reversing the process. There is no more boring job imaginable. I was with him one morning before work when he was rolling up the usual six joints that got him through the day. "Everyone smokes dope on this crew," he told me. "The other day the foreman told me he had a suspicion that a couple of the truck drivers were getting high. I didn't have the heart to tell him that they are all stoned, all the time. There's not a one of them that won't stop and chat and smoke a friendly joint with me."

Sylvia, under the table, had very little luck in eliciting a quiver or a twitch from my fucked out member. "Goodbye, sweet prick," she whimpered as she zipped me back up and dragged herself onto the chair. I was wondering what had become of Ace and whether I had missed my plane and thinking it was time to go to the john for another joint when I noticed that two airport security guards were looking warily at a joint that was lying on the floor about ten feet from our table. I instantly sobered up. "I think I dropped something," I whispered to Sylvia. Waves of paranoia poured over me.

"Don't worry," said Sylvia. "They can't do anything to you." Alaska of course has the most lenient marijuana laws in the United States, and I realized that ultimately I wasn't liable for anything more than a citation and a hundred-dollar fine, but the paranoia of a drug-addled pipeliner knows no bounds. Sylvia was out of her seat and following the guards to their station. She returned in a few minutes. "Routine," she said. "Right at this moment it seems to be a toss-up as to whether they'll fill out the forms on it or smoke it. Watch out for stoned security guards."

And so on Thursday morning, with the temperature forty-three below and the sun expected to rise shortly, I was lying on the floor at the airport and hoping that Sylvia and Ace would somehow shuffle my luggage through the line and get me on the plane. I knew that it would take me several days to recover from the horrendous things I had done to my body in the last three days, but since I was going to work on the pipeline I had nothing to fear. I thought how nice it would be if there was a severe drug shortage in the camp, but that is never to be counted on. Back in the early days of the pipeline there were sometimes not enough drugs to go around, but that was because many of the laborers went to the camps expecting to work and thinking that there would be no time for debauchery anyway.

But too often that turned out not to be the case, and now no self-respecting hippie laborer will go to camp without his stash, any more than a self-respecting Louisiana pipewelder is going to show up without a case of his favorite whiskey. If you can't drink it all yourself it's always a hell of a way to make friends.

The plane got off the ground only half an hour late, which is pretty remarkable considering the circumstances. I wasn't the only drunken, stoned pipeliner trying to make his way aboard. It's damned hard to look forward to a month or nine weeks of work with no bars and very few women and no solace but a paycheck. And that's what going to the Slope is all about.

The fellow sitting next to me on the plane was sympathetic when he saw my condition. "Hard night?" he asked.

"God, yes," I moaned. "My old lady made me stay up and fuck all night. I'm beat."

He laughed and nudged the guy next to him, apparently an equipment operator by his looks. "This guy had to stay up and fuck all night," he told him. "Ain't it a hell of a life?"

"Sure is," grunted the equipment operator. He pulled a bottle out of his parka. "Maybe a little tequila would fix him up."

"Oh no," I moaned, "No more drinking."

"Ah, come on," he urged, "It's good for what ails you."

"Okay," I said, "but only one."

The Men and the Work
and the Northern Mystique

The North Slope in winter is like nothing so much as the moon. It has a few essentials that the moon is missing—air, water, a slightly more agreeable climate—but for the most part you have to bring your own life-support system with you. Eskimos, of course, have lived here for centuries, but they have knowledge that it took them centuries to acquire, and ways of doing things that are perfectly adapted to their specific environment. Even with their great knowledge, they lived hard lives and the threat of death by starvation was ever present. If you're a white man you might as well be on the moon.

In the wintertime it is unendingly white, the whole country covered with snow ranging from a few inches to several feet deep, depending on the drifts. There are almost no landmarks. Pingoes, little hills of ice thrust up by the heaving of the ground as it freezes and thaws, can be seen if you're no more than a few miles away. On a clear day the Brooks Range, eighty miles to the south, is visible. Other than that there is nothing distinctive to be seen, save the oil wells, buildings, and roads of the pipeline.

The land is amazingly empty in the winter. A few misguided caribou will spend the dark days there, for some reason not having migrated south with the herd. They paw through the snow and eat the moss that insulates the ground and keeps it frozen year round. Occasionally you see a raven, the hardy bird that shows up wherever there is garbage. There are foxes with gleaming fur, Arctic foxes that like to hang around the camps for the free food; sometimes you see a fox, more often you see their tracks. There are wolves too, but wolves are shy and seldom show themselves. These animals are spread out widely across the country; the land won't support dense populations.

In the winter it gets cold, though the extremes are no colder than in the interior of Alaska. But there is the wind and the dark. Prudhoe Bay sits near the 72nd parallel, five degrees inside the Arctic Circle, and the sun does not shine there for over two months. In the summer, of course, the sun stays above the horizon continuously for over two months. The land of the midnight sun is the land of the noonday moon. Although the sun doesn't come up, there is a bit of ghostly light each day, even on the twenty-first of December. A short pre-dawn is followed by a short twilight and then it's dark for another twenty-one hours.

The wind blows incessantly. There are no mountain ranges to channel it, so it blows east-west, sometimes clipping along at forty knots or more, very infrequently dropping off to calm. In the summer you want the wind to blow—it keeps the mosquitoes down. There is nothing in the natural environment to stop the wind, so the unnatural obstacles, the raised roads and buildings, bear the brunt of the drifting snow.

The Arctic is a desert, or very close to one. If it weren't for the permafrost (the perpetually frozen ground that holds the water on the surface) the Arctic would look like parts of

Arizona or New Mexico. It gets only about three inches of precipitation per year. As it is, these three inches stay near the surface, so that there are large rivers, hundreds of creeks, and, in the state as a whole, 3 million lakes that are larger than twenty acres. In the winter, of course, everything in the Arctic is frozen and covered with snow, so the water can't be distinguished from the land. Not even the Beaufort Sea is discernible under the drifted snow, looking only like more of the same. From any of the camps at Prudhoe Bay you can look out on the bay, but in wintertime it looks no different than the land.

I was in Prudhoe Bay for weeks before I learned to feel in any way comfortable with this setting. It is utterly alien, much more so than an expanse of desert or prairie. When I first arrived there in January the sun was hidden behind the curve of the earth, and to make it even worse I hit a cloudy period.

Even when daylight comes it doesn't clearly mark the southeast, where the sun begins to rise once again toward the end of January. With clouds diffracting the light it is hard to tell which side of the sky is brighter. I never could get my directions straight.

When the sun first begins to peek out after its two-month rest, it appears as the glass globe of an old-fashioned floor lamp, hugging the horizon. Even then directions are difficult to determine. The sun swings in a short arc and then it is dark again. But day by day it rises higher in the sky, and although there are sure to be dark days, the daylight is ever increasing. About the middle of March you can even begin to feel optimistic about spring.

If the oil is to be gotten out of the ground and shipped south, that job has to be done by men (and a few women) and it unfortunately has to be done in Prudhoe Bay. What kind of man is it who will enter this alien place and begin to do the job that he is experienced in doing in Louisiana or Texas?

A partial answer to this question can be given by listing the various sorts of work that have to be done, and the union that handles each line of work.

The Teamsters are known as truck drivers, but in reality they do a good deal more than that. One out of every ten members of the Alaska work force is a Teamster, and they are unquestionably the most powerful union in Alaska. Among the Teamsters are included not only truck drivers, but bus drivers, warehousemen, forklift drivers, clerical workers, and surveyors. The Teamsters have simply been there to organize anyone that wanted to be organized, and probably more than any other group, they have profited from the pipeline.

The building construction people also figure heavily in the work force. Carpenters, electricians, plumbers, iron workers, sheet metal workers, and laborers are all needed to build and maintain the camps. To cook the food in the camps and keep them clean, the Culinary Union provides cooks, helpers, and bullcooks (the camp version of a maid). All rooms are cleaned daily, the only item that a worker has to attend to being his laundry.

When it comes to construction of roads and the pipeline right-of-way, it is the Operating Engineers who handle the equipment. Except for forklifts in warehouses and certain small drills, which are run by laborers, the operators run all the equipment—drills, backhoes, draglines, front-end loaders, Cats, sidebooms, cranes, etc. The laborers supply powdermen, or blasters, as well as the usual toters and diggers.

But the group most essential to pipeline building is the pipeliners, coming from the Pipewelders and Fitters Union, which has its only local, #798, in Tulsa, Oklahoma. The pipeliners work with the pipe—they position it, weld it,

X-ray the welds, test it, and have a hand in installing the supports beneath it.

The 798ers, as they are called, are a living myth. They are known as the roughest, toughest, least-willing-to-take-any-shit-from-anyone, meanest, drinkingest, fightingest union that you'd ever hope to lay eyes on. The Teamsters may have power, the ironworkers may have high wages, but the 798ers have it made. There are only about 5,000 men in the pipeliners' union, and they have a virtual monopoly on the business, or at least they act like they do.

798ers are to a man southerners. They grew up in the south, they do most of their work there, and they like to think that wherever they go they bring home right along with them.

You can spot a 798er from a mile off. Whether they weld or not, and many of their jobs have nothing to do with welding, they wear multicolored cloth caps with short bills that can be put on backwards in case the wearer wants to slip a welder's helmet over his head. They wear cowboy boots and jeans. They have short hair. They are almost all country boys, most have not gotten very far in school, and speak strictly Southern English.

And so far as I know they are all white. I have heard rumors that there are black pipewelders, or at least black apprentices, but I never saw one—there for damn sure aren't very many. As a Mississippi welder once told me, "I don't know whether there are any niggers in the union right now, but up till a few years ago there sure wasn't. And you have to give the Klan a lot of credit for that." The pipeliners are dinosaurs, a tiny group of men that survives by having as its specialty a miniscule bit of technological expertise. But, son, them boys can flat weld pipe!

Even with the Alaska-hire policy, which for at least the first two years of the pipeline was not very stringently enforced, the workers who are from the lower 48 (as the rest of the United States is known in Alaska) are probably in the majority. As I have said before, the laborers are solidly Alaskan. The Teamsters have a good number of Alaskans in their ranks, but also huge numbers of truck drivers from the northwestern and central United States. There were a lot of Alaskans already in the building trades, and so, many of the plumbers, electricians, and carpenters are from Alaska. But the hard core pipeline builders—the 798ers to be sure, and the specialty equipment men, such as sideboom operators—are southerners. A major pipeline had never been built in Alaska before, and so Alaskans did not have the requisite skills; nor did anyone seem interested in teaching them.

The way that the various groups relate to each other cannot be described as outright war, although it has sometimes come to that, nor as friendly and peaceful, though strong friendships are often made and sometimes continued. There is a certain amount of clannishness—the pipeliners stick together because that's the way they do things, and the pipelining hippies stick together because they haven't got any other choice.

The first tenuous communications between these two groups take place in the warm-up shack. Pete the welder winks at Jack the sideboom operator: "You know, I reckon the reason these fucking hippies never get any work done is because they're stoned all the time on that there marijuana."

"I reckon that might be true," allows Jack.

And there might be one especially adventurous laborer or Teamster who'll say, "Well, at least we don't come to work with a hangover."

And then the argument begins. Sometimes it takes place as friendly banter, and sometimes it can get downright nasty. There are a multitude of issues to be wrangled over. Two diametrically opposed lifestyles collide. There is the question of race. Southern pipeliners are divided evenly between simple racism, which is so common that you get used to it, and good old down home pickhandle swinging bigotry. On the other side are those who just generally believe that blacks or chicanos are the same as anybody else and find the constant racist statements intolerable. It can get vicious.

In 1975, down at Tonsina on the southern half of the line, a bus driver was beaten and left unconscious in a ditch when he defended the right of a black laborer to sit wherever he wanted on the bus. The pipeliners were insisting that he go to the back of the bus. The Teamsters walked out for three days and several men were arrested.

In another incident two laborers took on half a busload of pipeliners, lashing out with two-by-fours as the men one by one exited from the bus. Individual fights are common, and would be much more so if there weren't a strong prohibition against fighting on the job. Anyone who gets into a fight is automatically fired, so the workers at least think twice before throwing any punches. That's official policy, at any rate.

But violence abounds. A friend of mine reported that on a crew working between Fairbanks and Livengood, it was the practice of the 798ers, as a sort of initiation rite, to pull down the pants and grease the balls of laborers who happened to invade their territory. The 798ers had a warm-up shack with a sign on the door permitting entry only to workers belonging to their union. Anybody who went near this shack was subject to retaliation. My friend, a six-foot-four-inch mountain man who stays in top physical condition and is absolutely fearless, was the only non-pipeliner member of the crew who escaped routine harassment. He was known as "Bearclaw" because of the necklace of grizzly bear claws that he wore. He would explain, fingering the two and a half inch long claws, "I don't like to kill, but this bear came after me and it was either me or him. I take care of myself." They left Bearclaw strictly alone. I experienced the end of harassment after I took to carrying around a number two sand and gravel shovel and letting it be known that I considered the tool of my trade a dangerous weapon.

Since there are a multitude of issues to argue about and seemingly endless idle time to fill up, we argue. There's no problem choosing up sides: it's rednecks versus longhairs. Although long hair has been around for a long while now and generally carries no political significance with it, to a pipeliner it is a red flag. As blacks were systematically excluded for so long from pipelining, so were longhairs. By outright violence and lesser harassment, pipeliners made sure that there would be no longhairs working on pipelines. Even short-haired men with beards formerly didn't meet the test.

And so the hostilities rage. There is pot smoking versus drinking, welfare, political candidates, and even heated arguments about the correctness of the Vietnam War. Of course, many of these arguments are caused by the frustration of being in a place where there is nothing to do but work and sometimes damned little of that. And as with cowboys and Hells Angels, there is the group mentality, the attitude which says, when you're together with others of like persuasion you present a united front.

I might appear to be the mortal enemy of any and every southern pipeliner. That's not the case at all. As individuals, the rednecks that I so often nearly came to blows with proved to be as friendly as anyone I would ever hope to meet. In actuality we were both fighting the same battles and had the same interests. We both wanted to get through the day, collect our paychecks, and do the best job that we knew how to do. And we had lots of other common interests, if we could just get around to talking about them.

I grew up on a farm, and most pipeliners have done a little farming at one time or another. When we started talking about raising hogs or harvesting wheat we could get along just fine. And I found that guys who had just denounced me as a "low down faggot communist scum" would give me hours of their time telling me about the intricate details of various phases of pipeline building—the welding, spacing, stabbing, or whatever. And sometimes, if we happened to share a bottle of bourbon while we talked, we even got to be friends. I found that matters were not so serious as they sometimes seemed.

I told a welder friend of mine about a mechanic that I'd just stood nose to nose with, shouting for all we were worth. "Oh, don't worry about him," said Elton. "He's just an overgrown country boy who'd like to think he's tough, and in a couple of years he'll probably get religion and that will be the end of it." (I promised Elton, who was the best damned welder you'd ever want to see, that if I ever got round to writing a book about the pipeline I'd put him in it. Keep the faith, brother!)

In order to understand the situation that exists in the camps along the pipeline, it is necessary to have a look at what it's like for a pipeliner to come to Alaska and go to work. Especially if he gets his job in the middle of the winter, he's going to experience some major cultural shock.

He gets on a plane in Dallas, Flight 798, the Pipeliner Special, where it's seventy degrees and the sun is shining. Seven hours later he lands in Fairbanks, where it's fifty below and most likely dark, and he falls immediately into the clutches of the Alyeska bureaucracy. He figured it would be cold, but not this damned cold, so he hasn't got enough clothes to stay warm. He gets on a bus that travels down Airport Road to Fort Wainwright, where after a considerable wait and having identified himself half a dozen times, he is assigned a room for the night. So far he's seen nothing but snow and lights shrouded in ice fog.

He's confident. He has gone to strange places and built pipelines before and he by god knows—something very few people know—how to build pipelines. He's confident, but he's been cold ever since he arrived. It's cold in the bus— they don't make heaters to keep a bus perfectly warm at fifty below. The windows are frosted over, and the metal handles on the door will give you immediate frostbite if you touch them with bare hands.

The pipeliner does what he knows how to do in a strange place: "Hey, where does a guy go to have a good time around here?" So he heads to a bar, staring in disbelief when the bartender looks at the dollar bill lying on the counter and says, "Come on, come on, a beer is a buck and a half here!" And if he stops to talk to one of those pretty girls lining Second Avenue, he's in for another shock: "A hundred dollars for a piece of ass! You must be out of your mind!"

She's not. That's the going rate. "You can go back to Texas if you don't like it, cowboy," she says. "Nobody asked you to come here."

The next morning he is herded, hangover and all, through orientation. He sees vivid shots of frostbitten fingers, black and swollen, and a pretty film about Alaskan natives, and some P.R. hype about the pressing need for Alaska oil. The information he is given about how to survive at fifty below or more is good, reasonable, and trustworthy, but there's not nearly enough of it. At the end of orientation he gets a physical examination and a chance to purchase some of Alyeska's fine cold weather gear. Well, at least it looks fine.

There's a huge, wonderful down parka made of a guaranteed fire resistant, rip resistant, water resistant covering with goose feathers inside. The only thing the shell is not guaranteed against is leaking feathers, and feathers it leaks in huge quantities. The zipper has a life expectancy of about three weeks. I once worked with a crew that had to threaten to walk off the job before Alyeska got them some new parkas. Seems that fourteen of them had fine down parkas that would no longer close in the front.

The rest of the equipment is also of inferior quality or inferior design. The down pants are fine (they too leak feathers) when you're standing still but as soon as you start to work they are too hot. The mittens are too bulky to work in. The insulated boots—Sorrels—are the best that can be bought commercially but are not as good as the Army surplus boots that most Alaskans wear. This weird looking foot gear, known as bunny boots, have over the last five years increased in price from five dollars to a hundred or more. The question is not how much are they worth? but rather, how much will a man pay for warm feet?

When the pipeliner has gotten through orientation and perhaps wandered around Fairbanks for a while, constantly being shocked at the prices and the assertions of the merchants that he can go home if he doesn't like it, he is put on a bus to the airport and shipped to a pipeline camp. Here he meets more bureaucratic procedures and a place even more foreign to him than Fairbanks. Small wonder then that he's glad to get together with some fellows of like mind and talk things over.

Everywhere he turns he meets frustration. He comes to the camp totally unprepared to deal with the realities of the work, the weather, and the people he has to deal with. Longhairs cook his food, hold his welding rod, drive his bus to the work site. They know the ropes, they know about the weather, and they're in the majority. There are very few women in the camps and the ones that are there are almost certainly Alaskans, and for the most part natives. They don't respond kindly to a drawled construction worker come on. It will probably take him a while to get a roommate that he likes. The people who assign the rooms in the camp have an uncanny ability to team up the most impossible room partners. Future rock-and-roll stars, after dragging guitar and amplifier all the way from Phoenix or Fairbanks, find themselves sharing a room with a sixty-eight-year-old cook who has to get to bed by seven o'clock, doctor's order. Quiet readers try to settle down next to all-night poker games. Blacks ordinarily get stuck in rooms with nigger haters from Little Rock. Those who are minding their own business and trying to write a book about the pipeline get matched up with middle-aged men who are sadly and vocably unsuccessful at love. Pipeline marriages never work.

If the Southern pipeliners are a bit clannish, it is not surprising. They are merely taking care of themselves as best they know how. Even at work, where they are doing what they do best, there are tremendous frustrations. Life is much different with the mercury hanging in there at forty-five below. The clothes you must wear make you inefficient, and of course it's hardest the first couple of weeks that you wear them. Every winter I have to relearn how to do such simple things as tie knots with my mittens on and light a cigarette with one mitten off in the shortest possible time. Jesus, you are inviting frostbite every time you take a piss!

The severe cold makes a difference in almost everything that has to be done outside. Until you learn how to act, you've got to be aware of the cold at every moment, or you can get hurt. Until you've got it firmly in your subconscious that you don't touch metal barehanded, you're in danger.

Because of the environmental conditions, working on the Alaska Pipeline is radically different from working on any other. As a foreman told me one day, "I know how to build pipelines, but I don't know how to build this goddamn line. It's a whole new ballgame." To a worker who is not completely aware of the ecological problems involved, the prohibitions against running a Cat over the tundra or dumping some oil on the ground seem idiotic, and furthermore, they slow him down.

It is a tradition in the construction industry that when you rest, you rest, and when you work, you by god work. You might not be too concerned about holding your coffee break to fifteen minutes, but when you're working, you want to get the job done. It's a matter of pride.

Although I am completely in favor of the environmental regulations that are being enforced in the building of the pipeline, they do certainly slow things down. They're necessary, but a pain in the ass. The professional pipeliners, who have never worked under these conditions before and are mainly concerned with getting the job done, often take the regulations as a personal insult. The inspectors who enforce the rules have occasionally feared for their safety.

No matter what the difficulties involved, the pipeliners keep on working. This is not to say that some of them don't leave after they've been in camp a week or two—and there are a good number who during the last couple of years have simply refused to get off the plane when it set down at the camp runway. But by and large they stay. Sooner or later they adjust to the life of the camp, or at least adjust to having seven or eight hundred dollars a week coming in. They grouse and bitch about conditions and taxes and hippies and having to pay their way back and forth from home to Fairbanks every nine weeks, but they stay. They work because they are workers, because they have always worked—and because no matter how much you happen to dislike your situation, it's damned hard to turn down the kind of money you can make on the pipeline. Although there is constant talk of walking off the job and complaints that the unions sold out when they agreed to a no-strike contract, there hasn't been much work in other parts of the country, and you can't beat the wages. So they keep on pipelining.

With the Alaskan contingent it's a completely different situation. The laborers are notorious for being as unreliable as a work force could ever get. One of the reasons is something that I mentioned earlier: many people chose to live in Alaska because it offered an opportunity to be free of working for other people. At most a job is a three-months-out-of-the-year proposition. And so when they go to work on the pipeline it isn't because they want to make a career out of pipelining, it's because they want to make a few of the quickest, easiest bucks they can manage. At $11.10 an hour, the pipeline looks like the perfect place.

The professional pipeliners have problems adjusting to Alaska, and Alaskans have problems adjusting to the pipeline. The young, independent Alaskan, beyond a careless curiosity, has no interest whatsoever in pipelines, and even less interest in working on one. Whether the pipeline ever gets built or not is immaterial to him. There's no appeal in working for someone else, and certainly no appeal in going to some godawful ticky-tacky camp where you have to be sneaky about smoking dope and try to get along with a bunch of rednecks.

Whereas the southern pipeliners are working for a living and doing their job, the young Alaskan usually sees going to work as an evil necessity that is going to take him away from his real work—gardening, housebuilding, reading, writing, or whatever. He has no feeling that he is accomplishing something useful, and is very likely to feel that he is doing something that ought not to be done at all. While he could get behind a massive project that he thought was for a human good, and would probably work for nothing on such a project, he definitely can't get behind the pipeline.

The laborer usually goes to work in order to get enough money to buy something that he wants—lumber for a house, a truck, a stereo, a pound of weed to spend the winter with. He works grudgingly or cheerfully or any other way he can figure out to get through the evil time, and then he quits. Laborers (and others who fit into this category) are constantly quitting, quitting with or without notice, dragging up for any reason at all and going home.

There is also the matter of the cost involved in going to work. When a man from Alabama quits a job he has to pay for a plane ticket to Alabama, and then buy another one to Fairbanks if he wants to come back to work. If you live in Fairbanks or Anchorage you get a free plane ride home. Shit, some people will take a job just because they feel like going for a plane ride. Big fun, fly over the Brooks Range, do your laundry in the camp, snag a couple days' pay, and fly home again.

And since men are constantly and lightheartedly quitting, there are always a lot of jobs available. It turns into a sort of shuffle. Somebody drags up at the Livengood Camp, and a guy who just quit at Cold Foot takes his place and then somebody who quit at Dietrich takes *his* place and so on. It's creating jobs, man, solving the unemployment problem. There are even a good number of "camp hoppers" around, who take a job without any intention of working at that job. They show up, do nothing, stick around until they get fired (which can sometimes take a couple of weeks on the slacker crews), collect their pay and go get another job. Even if you get fired the first day out, you're making money, what with travel time, "show-up time," and all the other money-making schemes that are necessarily part of the contract but rather easily taken advantage of.

There are those who say that this kind of activity is positively disreputable, against all notions of fair play, and the reason that this country is going to the dogs. What does our pipelining hippie have to say to that?

"Fuck the pipeline! I used to have a nice little homestead up on the Steese Highway and now there are two hundred trucks a day rumbling by my door. Did they play fair with me?" And then too there is another thing to consider. While it might seem unkind to quit a job, or especially to quit without notice, it would seem equally unkind for the contractor to lay a worker off, though no one would ever assert that the employer didn't have a right to do this. If the worker is somewhat ruthless, the company is even more so. If a contractor wants someone to work for him for two days, he hires him and then lays him off when he doesn't need him anymore, and that's that. No one ever apoligized to me for laying me off.

The natives who work on the pipeline are in a class all by themselves when it comes to being unreliable. Once again, there are many who have been working on the pipeline since the day it began and will continue working on it until there's no more work to do. But for the most part, they represent an extreme case of non-participation in "the American way of life." To many of them, holding down a job is an utterly alien concept, especially to those who are carrying on the age-old tradition of living off the land. They don't need a lot of money, and having more than you need is obvious silliness. And so the natives, who are incredibly hard workers, will often go to work until they have the money for a new snow machine (the favorite reason for working) or a set of traps, or a new gun or canoe, and then quit. Along with the pipelining hippies, they will also quit because they are horny or because it seems like a good time to go fishing. I agree that both those things are more important than building pipelines.

I want to make it clear that I am speaking in very great generalities when I write about such groups as natives, Alaskan workers, and southern pipeliners. There are assuredly many who would not recognize themselves in my descriptions at all, and who would be offended at being included in them. There are Alaskan longhairs who work steadily year in and year out, there are philosopher pipeliners, there are many clear exceptions to any of the groups I have described. There are as many reasons for working on the pipeline as there are men who have worked on it. In actuality I don't say this out of any sense of journalistic fairness, I just want to make sure there aren't any mean sons of bitches throwing punches at me while pointing to this page next time I'm broke and have to go to work.

If there are any people working on the pipeline who have a "bad attitude" (yes, that's what they call it), it has as much to do with working conditions as with the prejudices and lifestyles of the workers. It is outrageously frustrating not to be able to do any work, and that is exactly the situation on the pipeline. This is not to say that we don't earn our money—we do. I sure as hell wouldn't sit around in a twelve-by-sixteen warm-up shack somewhere outside of Five Mile Camp with ten other men for any *less* than a hundred dollars a day. But the amount of work that I have done on the pipeline, even though I have been more than willing to work, is negligible. I always find it hard to make people believe that pipeline workers actually don't do very much work. Those who aren't aware of the situation think that I must be telling tales—how can it be that the highest paid workers in the world don't work? *Who's building the pipeline?*

The answer to these questions is rather complicated. First of all, there are a certain number of workers on the line who are busting their asses. Certain equipment operators for instance, the backhoe operators in the ditching phase, where the ditch is being dug out for the pipe at the rate of a mile a day—generally work hard. There is one man to run one machine, and he runs it until he breaks something. Fortunately the old backhoes break regularly.

But along with this backhoe comes an oiler, whose duty is to keep the machine greased, keep the windows in the cab clean, and assist in lining up the backhoe on the ditch. Since he is an apprentice operator at the same time that he is an oiler, he is theoretically learning how to run the backhoe.

While the operator works all day, the oiler is lucky if it takes him two hours to perform his tasks. He would consider himself lucky if it took longer. If he works two hours a day, there are eight more of standing around, reading a little, trying to stay warm, getting stoned—whatever it takes to waste those eight hours of enforced idleness. Oilers aren't lazy, there's just very little for them to do. And every backhoe, every dragline, every crane, every drill on the line has to have an oiler.

On this same ditching crew there will be several mechanics, who are obviously necessary if the machines are going to be kept running. With mechanics it's either feast or famine. When the machines are cantankerous, they will bust their asses to fix them; when the machines are humming, they sit.

Besides those who should presumably be working but aren't, there are also a few men on the crew who were never intended to accomplish much, but have to be there anyway. There are foremen, who may or may not be needed, and scads of supervisors who drive by once a day to swap tales with the foremen. And then there are inspectors of one kind and another. The geologists, or dirt-squeezers, as they are known, every half hour get out of their truck and test the consistency of the soil. Another inspector occasionally drops a tape measure in the ditch to see if it is deep enough. There also has to be a bus driver to take the crew back and forth to the worksite, and once he's on the job there is little to do but wait for quitting time.

And then there are the laborers. I worked as a laborer on a ditching crew one time, and I never did quite figure out what I was there for. I helped replace broken cables when that was necessary, and sometimes I pounded in stakes along the path of the ditch, a sort of elementary surveying operation. There were about a half a dozen of us, and for the most part we got stoned with the oilers. And sat around.

Drank coffee. Read a little. Bullshitted with the boys. Argued about sex, dope and the Vietnam War. Ate doughnuts. It was dull. I quit.

There is a certain romance and satisfaction about working hard and being strong. You don't want to work like a slave, but like a man. You want to be able to bitch and grouse about how hard you work, and be tired at the end of a day. I have had a couple of jobs where that was possible, if only for a short while, and it made the days easier to get through. The more a crew is idle, or the more it is given little made-up jobs to do so that it doesn't appear idle, the worse morale gets. I once sat with a crew in Prudhoe Bay for weeks when we would have occasional bursts of work, but for the most part there was very little to do. As time passed, it began to seem harder and harder to get out into the cold and do the little bits of work as they came along. We became the surliest, most rebellious crew that a poor bossman from Louisiana ever had to try to get any work out of.

At first we sat around wishing that there was some work to do. We talked about what we'd do if there was some honest work. There was constant banter about whether the longhairs on the crew *could* work or not, providing there was something to do. We'd work for an hour and talk about it for five. A full day of work looked so inviting. But for one reason or another the work didn't come. To begin with, there were about three times as many of us as were needed, and then the crew that was working ahead of us broke down, and the engineers couldn't seem to get it together, and there was bad weather.

After three weeks of this we decided that we simply didn't want to work. Instead of everyone going out into the cold when there was a task to accomplish, we'd send one or two guys out, taking turns. We posted an "unemployment list" on the wall and when you worked, your name went to the bottom of the list. The foreman was informed that he was to call out laborers from the top of the list. Those at the top of the list would go off and sleep in the bus or go into camp and take a shit six times a day. Our patient foreman, who was much in fear for his job, asked me one day, "Ed, don't you think it's kind of suspicious when twelve men all have to take a shit at the same time?"

"Well, Larry," I said, "nature works in strange ways."

Without getting into any psychological nonsense about motivation and reinforcement and such-like, it is true that the less you work, the less you feel like working. The hardest workers are people who work all the time—give them a day of work and it looks a lot like the last day of work and so they do it. But when you're not working, forget it. Sometimes on the pipeline the situation gets completely out of control.

When I took my first pipeline job I figured on working my ass off. For $9.60 an hour I was ready to do anything—lift hundreds of pounds, wrestle grizzly bears with one hand tied behind my back, leap tall buildings in a single bound, that sort of thing. I was impressed that somebody would pay me that kind of money and I intended to be worth every penny of it.

I had been on the job for less than four hours when I was rebuked for—of all things—getting too much done. "Don't kill yourself, Ed," cautioned the foreman, "you want to have something to do tomorrow, don't you?" From there on out all I heard was "Take it easy," and "Don't rush, we aren't going to get this job done in a day" and my favorite, "Ed, why don't you go hunt me up a nail stretcher." That, I figured out the second time around, was code for "Disappear for the rest of the day." Nail stretcher hunting time usually came around about two hours before quitting time.

My first job was in Fairbanks, renovating the buildings which became Alyeska's Fairbanks headquarters. I imagined that enforced idleness was the rule only in town, and that when I went to the Slope things would be different. They were. They were different because there weren't so many Alyeska people around, and since we were working miles out in the middle of a huge stretch of tundra, we could see them coming if they were going to inspect us. The second job was notable in that I took to calesthenics and jogging to keep from getting fat. By this time I couldn't bring myself to take the job seriously. It was slow going, not much happening, and all the time in the world to do what little we had to do.

I worked for an outfit that was putting in the feeder line, the pipe that takes the oil from the wells to the first pump station. This feeder line, mostly ten-inch pipe, can't be laid directly on the ground, but has to be set above the ground, propped up by supports which are known as bents. No one I ever talked to could give me an etymology of the word *bent*, but that is what they are called. We were known variously as the bent-setting crew and the bent setting-crew. At any rate, the bents consisted of pipe, twenty-plus feet long, half an inch thick and ten inches in diameter, set vertically in the ground with a beam of six-inch channel iron welded across the top. Five or six different feeder lines will be strapped together and secured to the supports.

Besides the engineering and surveying, the first project was to drill the holes eighteen feet into the frozen ground. All this activity must take place in the dark of winter; in the summertime the whole area is a quagmire and there is no possiblity of getting a drill into position to do the work. (For any equipment enthusiast who may be interested, the drill used is a specially built, beefed up Texoma 640 sitting on the back of a tracked carrier made by Bombardier of Canada. It is reportedly worth about a hundred and eighty thousand dollars. There are only thirty-six in existence.)

We worked in the dark. A portable lighting unit with a five kilowatt diesel generator (Onan) and four one-thousand-watt light bulbs turned the work area a sickly yellow. We stumbled around in the dark or semi-light, trying to locate survey stakes that were planted in the fall, before the snow came. After the drills had bored out their holes, a piece of plywood was thrown over the top to keep the snow out, and if there was a wind that plywood might have five feet of snow on top of it in a few days. We'd poke shovel handles through the snowdrifts, trying to hear the hollow plywood sound that meant we'd located one of a series of holes that a bent would go into. We'd flounder in the snow—sometimes the crust would hold and sometimes it wouldn't.

Jim and I called it "plywood mining." We worked way out ahead of the bent-setting crew; there was no chance of them catching us. We'd both worked on cost-plus pipeline jobs before, so we knew we didn't have to be serious about it and didn't have to produce very much. Just stay ahead of the bent-setting crew, preferably far enough ahead that we wouldn't be bothered by the noise of their crane and generators, and we'd be left alone.

Jim would poke a shovel handle into the snow, lean on it and drive it down. "I think I found some!"

"Plywood?" I shout back.

"Plywood!" he shouts.

I join him. "Do you think we ought to dig it out?"

"In my years of experience in the plywood mining business," he says (Jim's been on the job a week now), "when you find one piece of plywood you're pretty likely to find two or three."

After locating the plywood that covers the holes, we have to dig a square between the two holes, throwing out the gravel that the drills left behind. When we get down to the tundra (we don't have to dig into the frozen ground, so it's pretty light work, just shoving loose gravel aside), the skid setters will come behind us and stack up four-by-six skids to a specified height, and it is on these skids that the beam of the bent will rest. Although it sounds complicated, it is work that slightly trained monkeys could handle.

Jim and I dig on, moving enough to stay warm, every five minutes leaning on our shovels and talking. Jim came from Seattle and used to be a psychology student; I studied Greek and Latin. We know it's absurd, digging holes in the shore of the Beaufort Sea and talking about our respective scholarly achievements, but it makes the day go by. We have no interest in digging the holes, other than making our $10.35 an hour. We grin at the picture of ourselves digging holes at thirty-five below. But we keep digging, not very fast, just fast enough to stay warm. We keep digging, not knowing where the sun would come up if it took a notion to, not even knowing which direction the camp lies in, digging absurdly just outside the yellow light cast by the diesel generator and its thousand-watt bulbs.

But after a couple of weeks the plywood mining got mighty scarce. Troop morale was at an all time low. We'd work a little, smoke a little dope, sit around. Fewer and fewer people showed up for work. One day I decided it was time to go home. I told someone that I was going. Three days later eight laborers quit. So many people quit that Monday that the company had to charter a plane to get us all out of there. It was a major triumph.

Still, with all these goings-on, the pipeline is nearing completion. If it is true that there is very little work being done it is also true that the line will be finished in the summer of 1977. How is it accomplished?

Well, the fact of the matter is that there are probably four times as many men working on the pipeline project as there would be if it were what they call a "hard money project." For every man that is working there are three watching him. If there is a bit of work that requires one man, there are four workers to do that job. Inefficiency, poor planning, the cost-plus contract, cold weather, and union rules (allowing a man to do only one kind of work) all combine to make this one of the most monstrously wasteful jobs eveř undertaken. And the reason that it goes on this way is that no one really gives a damn. From the top to the bottom, no one is much concerned. People who buy gas and oil *ought* to be concerned, but Alyeska's PR men keep the consumers in their places. Going around looking for anyone who gives a damn is playing Diogenes of the north, and you'll have about as much luck as did that poor Greek truth-seeker.

It seemed that in the interlude between quitting one job and getting another, I always happened to read a newspaper article in which Alyeska's spokesmen said that they were aware that there was "a certain amount of waste and duplication in jobs," but they were at that moment doing something about it. And so I reasonably assumed that when I got my next job I'd be going to work. No more hour and a half lunch breaks, no more knocking off early, no more fucking around. When I got to camp I was amazed to see the changes that had been made. Instead of being able to grab a case of Cokes for your own private stash, you were now limited to two cans. The doughnut supply was also severely diminished. Hot lunches were cut out by a single blizzard of paper coming from the top, and there were fewer desserts to choose from. Sometimes there would be stringent timechecks to determine exactly what time the buses of workers were leaving the camp and returning to it from their worksites along the pipeline route. Which meant that we'd knock off an hour early and then drive slowly so as not to get to the gate too early. All the announcements were PR hype to appease the public, and had nothing whatsoever to do with production. What was saved in doughnuts was surely lost in having to hire more security guards to act as timekeepers.

The security guard timekeepers had a side effect that was not counted on. Placing a security station at the gate to a camp made it look like a forced labor camp—and we were already working in a place dangerously like Siberia. Whereas formerly we might have knocked off a little early, now we were certain to, if only to show the motherfuckers that they couldn't do this to us. If down home southerners and wild-eyed Alaska homesteaders have anything in common it is an ability to work on their own, and a distrust of those in power. The more power that Alyeska tried to exert over the daily lives of the pipeline workers, the more the whole thing became a game.

The pipeline always came shockingly close to being just like the army anyway. There were foremen who spoke of running a tight ship, and routine searches of rooms, and late night harrassment by the security guards. In almost every camp there have been incidents when people decided that they simply wouldn't put up with it anymore. In Prudhoe Bay seven pipeliners were drinking in a hallway when the camp manager wandered along. He ordered them to stop. They told him to go fuck himself. He said he was going to call a security guard. They asked him if he'd ever been gang raped. The bossman made the mistake of saying, "This is an order: either you stop drinking at once or I'll see to it that not a one of you has a job in the morning." Pipeliners don't stand for that kind of nonsense. The camp manager was swiftly deposited in a snowbank behind the camp. No one was fired.

Pipeliners are not the sort to stand by and see their freedoms denied. And there is no question about the method of protest to be used. It is swift, direct, and unmistakable. In Livengood workers objected to eating sandwiches that were prepackaged, days before, by non-union workers in California. The company was into another of its notorious red-herring money-saving projects. The protest took the form of overturning the tables full of sandwiches, breaking the tables, and directing threats at the food supplier. After dumping the tables the crew headed out for work, thirty miles away over a rough slow road. The trip took an hour and a half. Promptly at ten thirty the crew boarded the bus and came back to camp for lunch. At one o'clock they got aboard the bus and were back at the site by two-thirty. The next day there were fresh sandwiches.

Part of the reason that protests such as these can be effective is that the security guards in the camps are like everyone else: they get paid by the hour, not by the arrest. Some of them are former cops, and they can be mean. Some of them become very impressed with their power when they put on the ill-fitting blue or gray uniform, and they have to be put in their place. But for the most part the security jobs are filled by laborers—people just like me, who when it comes down to it are simply looking for the easiest way possible of getting through the day. They don't want trouble, and they aren't looking for it. More than one security guard has been known to take a restful toke of weed at the end of the day. But in order to understand the situation which exists, you have to know a little about the nature of pipelining and pipelines. There usually aren't any security guards at all.

Very few people know anything about pipelines at all, and I didn't before they started building one by my front door. Pipelining is a different world. It is part of the oil industry, and that immediately makes it different. Throughout the production end of the industry, there has long been a romance and a myth that is in large part justified. Among workers, the men who get the oil out of the ground and the men who build the pipelines are in a class by themselves. They have long been the highest paid workers, which immediately makes them special, at least in their own eyes. When you can make enough money in six months that it looks like a year's earnings, you have a kind of power that most people in the United States don't have—you can quit your job, any fucking time you want to. The oil companies have long done so well for themselves, pulling "free" oil out of the ground, that they could afford to spend a relatively large sum on production and still come out rich. It would seem that this is bound to come to an end, if for no other reason than that the oil reserves will be totally depleted by the end of the century, but a "get it while the getting is good" attitude still prevails.

Then too, there is a very American, cowboy-drifter sort of romance concerning the work itself. Oil is where you find it, and it's somehow much more exciting to say, "Mary Jane, I'm headin' off to Arizona. Gonna build me a pipeline," than to get up at six and drive to a Detroit factory, year in and year out. Pipeliners are always on the move, heading to a job in Texas or Kansas or Iran or Venezuela, and when the job is done or the itch gets to you, there'll be some new territory to conquer. A class-unto-itself develops, the pipeliners, and they have ways all their own. The same guys show up on every job, be it in Pennsylvania or California, and they get to know each other's quirks, learn to work together so that they can do ten hours' work in five hours, push a mile of pipe a day and have some time left over for a bottle of Jim Beam. Whole crews who worked together in Georgia also get together in Franklin Bluffs and get down to the business of pipeline building.

The contractor can afford to put up with a certain amount of fucking off, rough housing, drinking on the job, and other sins that would not be tolerated in any other workplace. Or perhaps it isn't that he *can* put up with it, but rather that he *has* to. Unlike most other workers, pipeline builders aren't expendable. Their bargaining power comes from the fact that despite all the ways in which they can coldheartedly and with calculation drive a contractor crazy, *they do know how to build pipelines*. And there aren't very many people around who do. It is exacting work, requiring a great deal of skill. It also happens to be very dangerous, and gets more dangerous depending upon the number of men on the crew who don't know what they're doing.

Almost anyone can learn in a relatively short time to handle a Caterpillar with a blade on the front, at least for non-critical work. But the operation of the machine that is used to handle pipe, the sideboom, which is essentially a Cat with an A-frame on one side, controlled by a series of cables, is not learned overnight. The typical sideboom will weigh in at around a hundred thousand pounds, of which about twelve thousand are counterweights that can be moved in or out at the operator's will, and are positioned on the machine opposite the load. A sideboom will appear completely mysterious to someone not aware of its function. There are cables running this way and that, a multitude of levers to control engine speed, counterweight position, boom and load cables, the winch on the back, and then the usual clutch and brake mechanisms. If the operator doesn't know where every one of them is, without looking and without hesitation, he'll probably kill someone before the morning's out.

A huge piece of pipe, each forty-foot section of it weighing three tons, will be lifted by half a dozen or more sidebooms all at once. They are positioned in a row alongside the ditch or, on the Alaska pipeline, along the above-ground supports. The ground is muddy, unstable, and treacherous. If one man makes the wrong move, if he doesn't support his share of the load, or if he tries to lift too much and snaps a cable, then the man next to him has a double load. If he can't handle it, he can be catapulted off his seat, thrown as his tractor tips, sailing through the air, hopefully to the other side of the ditch where he may have a chance of living. It can become a chain reaction, with all the tractors tipping and spilling the operators. The men working in the ditch don't have a chance. Working under a sideboom or, equally bad, a crane, is risky business at best.

I did a lot of it, and came to have the highest respect for the man who could handle his machine. Also an agonizing panicky feeling of terror when I saw one who couldn't.

The pipewelding crew—those who line the pipe sections up, space them to the proper distance, and finally weld them—endanger no other lives than their own, which are constantly in danger. Their real problem is that all welds have to be perfect—that's *perfect*. No bubbles, proper and uniform penetration, nothing overlooked. Anyone who is interested can learn to fire up a 200-amp Lincoln arc welder and stick two pieces of iron together. But when you get into pipewelding that won't do. Welders have an educated intuition about the iron—its temperature, its porosity. They *feel* it. They know the peculiarities of their machine and the particular welding rod they're using. It isn't a matter of sticking the rod on the iron and welding. The weld has to be perfect, and every weld is X-rayed to assure its quality. When a hundred miles of pipe is welded together, it becomes a hundred-mile-long pipe. The welds are stronger than the metal. When the "double jointing" (two sections of pipe are welded together with automatic welders in the pipeyard before they are scattered along the line) was started there was an early cutout rate of over 50 percent. That means that over half of the welds had to be cut out and done again. A poor welder doesn't last long. His job is on the line every time he picks up a "stinger" (the popular name for the positive electrode on a welder).

Out of the skill, out of the working together and drinking together and pulling down high wages, out of running the show and doing things the way they ought to be done comes the myth of the pipeliner. You drink hard, you work hard, you collect your pay and move on. Pipeliners don't take any shit, " 'cause Jack, if you want somebody else to do this job you just go ahead and try to find a man who can take my place." They repeat the old saw: "You can tell a

Texan, but you can't tell him much," then add, "and if he's a Texan pipeliner you can't tell him a *damn* thing." The myth of the pipelining rowdies got started because that's the way things were, and things stay that way because there's the myth to live up to.

When the pipeliners came to Alaska they brought their myths with them, right down to the pointy-toe boots that are flat guaranteed to give you a case of frostbite at anything colder than zero.

But Alaska was already a myth. It was the last frontier, the harsh romantic land of gold rushes, cold flat black in the winter and twenty-four hour sunlight in the summer, one man against the wilderness, free wild country where you could act any way you pleased and no one would blink an eye. The Alaskan myth lived, and the media always found it profitable to perpetuate the myth. For the newspapers and slick magazines and television the myth made money and wasn't, after all, that incredible. Log cabins still abound, even though they're more of an architectural style than the free place to live that they once were, and there are bears and wolves and soul-inspiring vistas. If the myth had started to die it was brought back to full life, even amidst the trailer courts and microwave communications.

The two myths—the myth of the pipelining fool and the Alaskan rugged individualist myth—went well together. The hard-drinking hard-working pipeliner could go to Alaska and do his level best to build a pipeline while fighting off bears, wolves, screaming wind, and cold like nobody had ever heard of before. Pipeline building was mysterious, and Alaska was mysterious, and it added up to a total mystique. Strange goings-on in the Land of the Midnight Sun.

Wherever there was money to be made, people got in on the act. Any restaurant in Fairbanks or Anchorage will serve you their pipeliner special, which if not any better, is at least bigger than anything else on the menu. From twenty-five ounce steaks to three eggs and ham with half a pound of potatoes, the pipeliner special is part of the menu. The airlines threw together the Pipeliner Special, Flight 798, non-stop Fairbanks to Houston. In Alaska, advertising ain't advertising unless it says something about the pipeline.

And the pipeliners believe it too. The pipeline, the Alaska Pipeline, that is, becomes all. Workers work with an awareness that, to quote commonplaces, "We're building the pipeline in Alaska. We're the highest paid workers in the world. We're making history." Sometimes it's said seriously and sometimes jokingly. A sideboom operator tells about his visits home while on R&R: "No, nothing too exciting this time. Same old parades, high school girls camped out on my lawn, tellin' it like it is to the Rotary Club and suchlike. I got tired of it, decided to come back and give you boys a hand."

It's not just the southern pipeliners who come to live the myth, by any means. Almost everyone is affected by it. You act as you are expected to act, like a little John Wayne of the north. If men coming back from the Slope act like wild men, it is partially because they are encouraged to act that way. Bartenders expect you to fight, women expect you to give them the hardest come on they ever got, and everyone expects you to spend money like it was going out of style. In many cases they get what they want, even from people who aren't actually disposed that way. It's damned difficult to take off your hardhat and start acting like a human being again.

While working on the pipeline the spirit of *machismo* prevails; it pervades every facet of life. You're either the "hardest working son of a bitch that ever had balls," or you're the "hardest bastard to get any work out of that the world ever saw." There are no compromises. The macho gets completely out of control, to the point where people who smoke cigarettes with filters are flirting with faggotry, and anything less than 86 proof is considered a "lady's drink." A pipeline camp is so thoroughly male chauvinist that women are regarded as having about the same value as a bottle of Jack Daniels, for entertainment purposes—only they cost more.

Women and sex are of course a constant topic of conversation in the warm-up shacks and dining halls, and more especially the women in the camp are talked about. The madonna-whore complex immediately damns any woman who sets foot in the camp: if she sleeps with anyone she's a whore, and if she doesn't she's frigid.

This pervasive machismo is one more thing that makes it difficult for the young Alaskan workers to put up with the pipeline. While most of us might not meet the tests of hard core women's liberationists (Alaska seems to bring out the more masculine virtues—in women as well as men) there are still many, myself included, who like to think of themselves as feminist sympathizers. But if one is going to think that way while working in a pipeline camp, he is either going to be very quiet or engaged in constant argument. And while it's a drag to listen to talk about hundred-dollar pussy and the natural inferiority of women all day long while saying nothing, it's also a hassle to defend the cause every time some slighting remark is made, which is about every three minutes. It is, of course, rather pointless to argue. Pipeliners aren't going to give women their due any more than they are going to think of blacks as equal to themselves. I once began a long-term controversy with a crew about whether women could do "men's work" or not. I happened to have with me a copy of *Ms* whose cover story was "Women in Sports," so I had lots of good information about the physical capabilities of women. While the points were granted one by one, it always became evident the next morning, when the controversy raged anew, that everyone had forgotten yesterday's facts and figures. Suffice it to say that pipeliners are hard core male chauvinists.

Attractive though the proposition may be, it is certainly ridiculous to blame the southern pipeliners for their invasion of Alaska. They after all do not want to be in Alaska at all. They would much rather be working in Louisiana, if there was any work to do there, and it is equally certain that most of them will be returning there when the line is built. Although it has proven a bad situation both for Alaska and for the men who came up from the lower 48, it is important to realize why they are in Alaska in the first place. They have been hired by Alyeska's subcontractors to build a pipeline. That's what they know how to do, that's their job, and they are most certainly going about it in the only way they know how. If anyone has invaded Alaska and trampled on the native population it is Alyeska, and not a bunch of guys who are only trying to earn a living. And one should not be surprised: the oil junkies will do what they have to to get their oil, and this is just one more thing they have done.

Weather

Alaska enjoys the distinction of being the coldest state in the U.S. Fairbanks has an annual mean temperature of about 25 degrees Fahrenheit. In January the mean temperature is minus seventeen degrees, and in July it is in the mid fifties. It isn't cold all year around, but when it is cold, it is colder than most people can imagine. To some large extent, it is the cold that makes Alaska what it is, in physical characteristics, population, and lifestyle. The very low density of population can largely be attributed to the cold—it seems that the people of the world have decided that they are willing to put up with deserts, but the Arctic is another matter. And while the inhabitants of any region on earth have to adjust to their environment, almost nowhere is that environmental adaptation so critical as in the far north.

In a warmer climate you can get away with a lot. There are many places in the United States where that sophisticated bit of shelter known as the house is largely a matter of convenience—it doesn't mean death if you don't have one. Where it is warm you can get lost in the woods for a few days and come away with nothing more serious than an empty belly. But unless a person is a completely qualified survival expert, he or she will almost certainly never be heard from again if lost in the Arctic winter. It is possible to survive, but mistakes will kill.

In different parts of the country, when people think of "really cold" they all think of different temperatures. In the midwest it might be zero, in Minnesota forty below, in northern California thirty degrees. In the northern two-thirds of Alaska the magic number is sixty below zero. Sixty below is about the coldest it will get for an extended period of time, say two or three weeks. It may occasionally dip to sixty-five or seventy below, but you don't worry so much about that. When you're engineering a house you think in terms of keeping it warm at sixty below; if it'll stay warm at that temperature you're pretty well set. When you buy a parka that's really more expensive than you wanted, the clerk assures you, "You'll be glad you have it when it's sixty below." When you put antifreeze in your radiator, you keep adding it until the bubble floats at sixty below. Minus sixty is a very important temperature.

To someone who hasn't experienced extreme cold, forty below is cold, and so is minus sixty. But to someone who has worked outside at both temperatures, there is a world of difference. I'll take forty below any day. If forty is cold, sixty is downright mean. Animals other than humans have sense enough to stay home at that temperature. A Husky curls up with his tail over his nose and waits it out. Bears are in hibernation. The caribou and moose have headed for the high country. Surprisingly, the higher the altitude, the warmer it gets, at about one degree per hundred feet. Up in the mountains it will rarely get more than thirty below. That's where the moose spend the winter.

At sixty below almost everything comes to a standstill. Nature seems to mount a conspiracy against motion. Water is frozen, and spittle is frozen before it hits the ground. Not so with urine, though claims have been made to the contrary. Water vapor freezes immediately, so you get ice on your mustache, ice on your eyebrows, and ice on the ruff of your parka. A dog will have a fine coating of ice all over its fur.

At sixty below you run into difficulties in breathing. You can actually frostbite your lungs by pumping too much cold air into them. Your throat can suffer the same malady. Part of the job of the sweeping hood and ruff of the Eskimo parka is to circumvent this problem. You walk about with a little tunnel in front of your face and produce a warm air pocket. In this way you not only warm the air that's going into your lungs, but you keep your nose and cheekbones, the two most likely areas to frostbite, from freezing.

But it is more complicated than that. When it's that cold, you absolutely have to keep moving in order to maintain body heat. You can't stand around at sixty below. If you must stay in one place, you have to dance, jump up and down, flap your arms, shiver a little, wiggle your toes and fingers, keep every thing in motion. That sounds tiring, but not impossible. But there's a catch. You can't move too much. If you get too hot, you sweat, and if you sweat, you freeze. You've got to move easily, just enough to keep warm, but not enough to perspire. The clothes that keep you warm do their job because they are *dry*; down is almost completely useless when it gets wet, and while wool retains some insulating value, it hasn't got enough for sixty below.

The slogan "Pipeliners never sweat" does not have its origin in the necessity to keep from perspiring in cold weather, but the effect is the same. Everything slows down in the intense cold of the Arctic winter, and people are no exception. For the native peoples it is a slow time of year, a time to lay back, make love, get fat, stay warm. Physics and metaphysics go together nicely. The cold dark days of winter are not meant for being active—animals know that, and people learn it. You can't hurry, you don't feel like it, and it is dangerous. When you breathe too rapidly you increase your chances of frostbite in the lungs, and you run the risk of getting wet by perspiring. On the job, you are also in danger of frosting your fingers if you should happen to touch metal without gloves on. You must learn to be slow, careful, methodical. After you've done it a while you act that way automatically, but at first it must be a conscious process.

Even the toughest bushwhackers and mountain men are susceptible to frostbite. It's a chance you take when you live in the wilds; if you happen to fall through the ice of a creek or have some kind of accident, you might get frostbite. But on the pipeline it usually happens through carelessness, through not being aware, through getting excited and insisting that the job must be done, no matter what. It's a lot of trouble to wear all the necessary protective gear, but if you try to substitute gloves for mittens at fifty below, you get stung, as a foreman of mine did, his first day on the job, while grabbing a piece of pipe. Often, the accidents happen soon after a man gets on the job. He wants to make a good showing, and he runs outside without his mittens, or without a ski mask, or with wet or untested boots, and within a few hours he's in the hospital. You have simply got to take care of yourself, especially if you haven't had much experience in cold weather. As you learn more you can cheat a little and get away with it, but by then you've outgrown the macho "I'm tougher than the winter is cold" bullshit. When it's seriously cold a good foreman won't push you, and if you want to keep all your fingers and toes, you won't let him. A Louisiana foreman who sits in his pickup all day long will sometimes try to make a crew live dangerously in cold weather, but he won't get very far.

But more often the problem is the exact opposite. The crew never learns to work in the cold at all. I account myself lucky that my first winter in the north I had a job that kept me outside all day long. I had to be out there, no matter what the weather. And then on the weekends I'd set out on foot to visit some friends who lived in a cabin ten miles out in the bush. I started in the fall and continued this all through the winter, never missing a day of work and never missing a weekend walk. As the days got colder and shorter I learned to cope with them, got the feel of the weather so that I could tell the temperature within ten degrees without a thermometer, learned how to dress, what to eat, and was able to experiment. I learned how to stay outside for long periods of time in extreme weather and without being uncomfortable. I once did my weekend walk at sixty-four below zero and suffered no ill effects, except that the woolen scarf I used to breathe through was a six-foot-long cake of ice by the time I got to the cabin. After I got there we drank some coffee, ate lunch, and then—went for a walk!

I really got to like cold weather, and although I never really came to prefer it to warm, I wasn't afraid of it or unwilling to live in it. It's an exhilarating feeling—perfect cold. Your body gets used to it, you learn that feeling a little cold isn't dangerous, and it can even be kind of nice once you don't blindly insist that you must be warm. And cold, of course, is relative—after a couple of weeks of sixty below, minus forty feels like spring. At minus forty you can unzip your parka! After you're outside an hour or so and get warmed up by walking, you can actually take off your mittens for a while. Winter gets to be big fun, time for playing in the snow, taking walks, going camping. Anything warmer than forty below comes to seem like ideal weather for working or playing.

On the pipeline it's a different matter. The strategy is not to get in tune with the cold, but to avoid it altogether. The idea is not to admit that this pipeline is being built in Alaska and get used to it, but to bring a little chunk of the lower 48 along. And so the camps are overheated trailer houses, the warm-up shacks are poorly insulated buildings heated with oversized stoves, and the philosophy is "stay warm."

It must be difficult as hell to face Alaska weather when you arrive in a pipeline camp in the middle of the winter. Your body is adjusted to a high-humidity fifty degrees above, and now it has to cope with a low-humidity fifty below. It's a tremendous shock when you haven't had a few months to get used to the ever decreasing temperatures. In this situation a person can't help but think of the cold as an enemy, a conspiracy against all that is right and sane. And so the fifteen-minute policy comes into play. Fifteen minutes working, and fifteen in the shack. Those fifteen minutes outside don't give you time to get warmed up. It is merely a matter of getting colder and colder and then running back inside to get warmed up.

In my experience it's the first hour outside that's the worst. If you stay outside an hour, and keep moving, you've got it made. Then you can stay out all day. But the companies can't afford to take chances with inexperienced men killing themselves out in the cold, and the only humane thing is to allow workers to come in and get warmed up anytime they claim they're cold. But if you go inside every time you feel cold, your body never learns to keep itself warm, and so all winter long, it's fifteen minutes in, fifteen minutes out.

Part of the problem too is the nature of the work. More than any other job, pipelining seems to require long periods of standing around. It's the laborers working with shovels who can keep themselves warm. Take it nice and steady, slow and easy, and you can dig all day long without getting cold and without sweating, which would make you cold. But the men who have to work with their hands, using a tape measure or fixing broken machines or any such stationary work, haven't got a chance. They're going to get cold, and that's all there is to it. They hate it, which is understandable.

It is understandable too that relatively little work is accomplished in the dead of winter. It is practically impossible to work efficiently; winter seems to have something against activity. It seems to be the nature of things to slow down in the winter. Besides the cold, it is dark. Darkness makes it difficult even to stay awake for long hours in the winter, just as the total daylight makes it hard to sleep in the summer. Those who have become accustomed to the environment tend to do most of their work in the summertime, often going sixteen or twenty hours a day, eating very little, just going full tilt, following the sun. And in the wintertime they lay back, sleep ten or twelve hours a night, eat a lot. Being out in the cold makes you tired and hungry. It takes an enormous number of calories just to keep warm. The meals in the camps are engineered to stuff five to six thousand calories a day down your gullet, and if you're working, you can eat that much without getting fat. But it is best if you gain a little weight at the beginning of winter—the fat adds some insulating protection.

Eating habits are an important part of dealing with the winter. You need extra carbohydrates, since they will be converted into heat to keep you warm. If you're hungry, you will almost automatically get cold. Since the insulation provided by clothing is not perfect, you are constantly losing heat, and if you cannot manufacture the heat to replace what is lost, you will develop hypothermia, which translated from Greek means "too little heat." When you're cold and you eat, you can notice an immediate effect. A little chocolate will warm you in a moment.

Given all these factors—the cold, which tires you and makes you inefficient, the dark, which is known to be depressing and slowing, and the necessity of carrying around twenty to thirty pounds of clothing all day long—it is small wonder that not too much gets accomplished by each worker in the wintertime. And besides the cold there is the wind. On the tundra of the North Slope, the temperatures do not often dip down to sixty degrees below zero. But it might as well be that cold, because the wind blows constantly. After a while there you get to think of ten miles an hour as calm. Twenty miles an hour is very common, and thirty or more is not unusual.

And here enters the wind chill factor. The chill produced by a combination of cold and wind is in many ways harder to deal with than simple dead cold, and it is more dangerous. I have never known the formula for calculating wind chill factor, but you can come close enough by subtracting two times the wind speed from the temperature. Thus, if it is twenty below zero, and the wind speed is fifteen miles per hour, the wind chill factor is fifty below zero. And although this is a calculation, that fifty below is just as cold as it would be if the temperature were fifty below on a calm day. On the North Slope these chill factors can get absurd. Try figuring out something like fifty below with a thirty mile an hour wind. It gets a bit ridiculous. I have actually been outside under such conditions, but not for long. When that happens work pretty well shuts down. In one way, the wind chill is not so bad as real temperature, because you can turn your back on the wind, and inside the hood of your parka it will be only the real temperature. But it can also be very dangerous, because if you took off your mitten when the chill factor was a hundred below, you'd be very likely to freeze your fingers.

The wind picks up snow and throws it at you. All over the Arctic are drifts of hard-packed snow, rammed into place by the wind. At thirty miles an hour there is snow swirling in the air, driving against anything that happens to get in the way. A road can be drifted over in half an hour. And the drifts of fine, dry snow are so hard that you can walk on them and leave footprints no deeper than you would in hard-packed dirt. It is these drifts that supply the "ice blocks" for building igloos.

If there is loose snow on the ground and the wind gets up around thirty miles an hour what is known as a whiteout can develop. You can't see at all, the air is simply full of snow. Whiteouts can happen very suddenly, and there have been a good number of workers trapped in them. There is no hope of going anywhere, you can't see the road or lights or your hand in front of your face. Men have been stuck inside vehicles or warm-up shacks for as much as three days until "she blew herself out." To the best of my knowledge no one has been killed, and I hope I'm right.

When a crew is caught out in a whiteout or a near-whiteout, that is known as a "weather day." Which means that you sit inside a warm-up shack or bus and wait. While this sort of inclement weather is occuring, it is permissible for the management to hold you at the camp and pay you for an eight-hour day, forty hours a week. That's all that's guaranteed when you go to the camp. But most of the foremen and their superiors are good fellows, especially when they too are getting paid by the hour. So in the morning there is an all-out effort to get to the worksite, no matter what the weather.

And then the foreman comes around. "Boys, we're gonna wait a couple minutes and see if this damn thing'll blow itself out. Now y'all stay inside, hear, cause I don't want none of you gettin' yourself killed." And so you wait, and look out at the weather, drink coffee, get high, pass around a bottle.

And after a while the foreman thinks of something that absolutely has to be done. He comes to the bus or shack. "Boys, we got some stacks of skids that absolutely has got to be covered up before the snow gets to them and we never see them till next spring." We troop outside to do the task.

And while we're out the foreman gets on his C.B. radio, calling back to the office: "Jack," he says, "I got these hands out working but they're having a hell of a time of it. Damn cold today. Could you give me a wind speed reading?"

Jack calls back, "Twenty-eight miles an hour, Sam, and I'd just as soon you kept them hands inside till this thing blows itself out. We don't want to lose anyone."

That's a weather day. If you show up at work you get paid for four hours. If you work five or more you get paid for eight. And if you stick it out till anywhere near quitting time you get paid for the full day, ten hours. I myself never lost an hour's time because of weather—that is not the case with everyone. Some camps have kept their workers in. And some camps have been full of mean drunk workers. You take your chances.

People do have hard times with the weather they have to work in while building the pipeline. But machines have an even harder time. While humans are tremendously a-daptable, machines are designed to operate under certain environmental conditions, and those conditions do not include temperatures of sixty below zero. It takes some ingenuity, some extra equipment, and a certain amount of luck to keep machines running at the extreme temperatures found in Alaska.

Consider the average American car. When the tempera-ture gets down around zero, even if the car is in good condi-tion, it begins to have problems. At zero it may start or it may not, depending on the condition of the battery and the weight of the crankcase oil. Now move it down the line to thirty below. Without some special precautions, it defi-nitely won't run. Most likely the engine won't even turn over. There are several problems. The common lead/acid battery loses most of its power at thirty below. 10-30 oil now has the viscosity of ninety-weight transmission grease. And the gasoline, if it isn't frozen in the line somewhere, won't explode as readily. If you should by some chance get that car started at thirty below, you'll find it very hard to drive. With a standard transmission you'll find it almost impossible to shift gears. The rear-end lubricant will be almost a solid mass of grease. The grease in the wheel bearings will be frozen too. The steering wheel will be very hard to turn.

Plop that same car down in sixty below and it'll stay right where you put it until it warms up. It's frozen solid, and if you tried to pull it with another vehicle that was running, the wheels wouldn't even turn, but rather skid along the ground.

However, machines do run at sixty below. Perhaps not very well or very much, but they run. It's complicated. Every fall, people in Alaska turn their cars over to service stations and garages to be winterized. The bill comes to one hundred-fifty or two hundred dollars. First of all you put in antifreeze that will take it to sixty below. But it can't be straight antifreeze—I mention this because most people don't know that unmixed antifreeze will solidify at low temperatures; it has to be mixed with water. After the radiator is taken care of you go around the car and replace all the oil in it with some of a lighter weight. You want it to remain in as near a liquid state as possible when it's sixty below. At the same time you replace the grease in the wheel bearings and other lubrication points. Next you install a circulating engine heater, which operates more or less like a coffee pot. It is hooked into a heater hose and then plugged into a source of electricity. This keeps the engine warm, and in Fairbanks it'll cost you about a dollar a night for the electricity to run it. Finally you must rig up some means of warming the battery. There are battery plates, battery blankets, or small battery chargers that will do the job. And then you're set, right? Well, sorta.

The problem is that no matter what you do, machines just aren't engineered to run at sixty below. Any plastic or rubber part will break very easily, and even steel becomes brittle. Last December when it was about forty-five below I was outside trying to get my Toyota pickup to run. I took the aircleaner off and set it down in the snow. My next move was to break one of those skinny hoses that are part of the emissions control systems. I adjusted the carburetor, picked up the aircleaner, slapped it against my knee to remove the snow and . . . it shattered. Lots and lots of little pieces of shiny plastic lying in my driveway. Hell of a way to learn that they make aircleaners out of plastic these days. The Alaskan naturalist fetish for materials like wood and steel comes from the fact that they work at fifty below. Anything made of plastic is going to break sooner or later.

Although keeping machines running through the winter is a pain in the ass, it can be done. But it is also very hard on the machine. Whereas in the warmer states an engine from Detroit will often run for a hundred thousand miles or more without a major rebuild, in Alaska you're lucky to get fifty thousand out of it. The reason for this is that each time you start it up in the winter, the oil does not begin to lubricate the internal engine parts until it warms up a bit. Thus, you are running your engine without oil for several minutes each time you start it cold. Everything wears out much quicker this way. It is decidedly in your favor if, when selling your used car, you can state in the ad "has never been through an Alaska winter."

And on the pipeline the situation deteriorates even further, since no one essentially gives a shit whether the machines run or not. As a matter of fact it's a lot nicer when they're not operating. You don't have to listen to them, smell their fumes, or work. The amount of down time on the machines is ridiculous. Everything that a mechanic every dreamed could go wrong does, and if he's not an experienced cold weather mechanic, a lot of things will go wrong that he never heard of before. Hydraulic hoses are constantly broken. Brake lines crack. Tires sometimes crack. Frozen gas lines and carburetors provide further challenges. Diesel engines, since they aren't damaged by idling as are gasoline engines, simply are allowed to run all winter long. They're a bear to start if they ever stop.

And when it comes to steel parts, they can be downright treacherous when it gets cold. Pins sheer that never would have otherwise. I once saw the mast of a Texoma 640 drill come tumbling down, ripping the parka off a lucky laborer, as a one and one-quarter inch steel pin sheered at fifty below. I don't claim to know the physics of this matter, but it does seem that the colder it gets, the more likely metal is to come apart.

There is almost never a day that goes by without loss of work time by broken equipment. This is referred to as "down time," and on the pipeline the time lost is outrageous. If the hydraulic hoses don't break, the seals blow, and if the machine will start then it won't run. When I was part of the Prudhoe Bay bent-setting crew, we were following a crew of seven drills. I don't remember even one day in two months when all seven worked all day. I was on the job a month before I even found out there *were* seven drills. I always thought there were five. There were several slow days when only one or two were running, and yet the mechanics were working twenty-hour days. The drill crews were doing calisthenics and staying high. Alyeska was issuing P.R. releases about down time and the price of oil going up.

Given the proper conditions, just getting to the job site can be a monumental task. When it gets really cold, the gravel roads are generally not slick, but they do get drifted in with snow quite quickly. In the morning we get into buses and trucks and head into a mass of swirling snow. The foreman goes first in his four-wheel-drive crewcab, calling out his discoveries on the C.B. radio to the buses or vans behind him. "Bus Number Two, you read me?"

"I read you, Honker. I don't know where I'm going, but I can hear you fine."

"Well, Bus Number Two, you watch out on the turn that's just in front of you. I almost didn't make it myself."

"Gotcha, Honker."

We continue on, the driver peering out his frosted window, trying to discern some trace of the road. The crew is betting on whether we'll make it or not. If we hit the ditch it's a matter of getting out the shovels and chains and seeing what we can do about the situation. Sometimes we end up with a whole convoy in the ditch. The four-wheel-drive crewcab gets stuck trying to pull the van out, and then the fuel truck sticks itself trying to get that out, and then the whole crew sits and waits till the mechanics can get a Cat running. I once saw a newspaper where a curious reader asked the editor, "Do you need an Alaska Driver's license if you only drive from one ditch to the other?"

Bus Number Two is on the radio. "Honker, did they plow that little access road over there?"

"Bus Number Two, I guess they musta did, 'cause nobody told me nothing."

The crew is betting that they didn't. And then it's time to turn onto the access road from the main road. "Bus Number Two, why don't you set yourself down for a minute, and I'll go survey this here situation."

Silence. The crew opens up the thermos' of coffee and gets out the doughnuts. The less inspired members don't even wake up. I got into the habit of foregoing my morning coffee so I could sleep through the boring forenoon hours.

Honker's radio crackles. "Come in? Anybody read me?"

"Uh yeah. How deep's that snow, Honker?" asks the bus driver.

" 'bout ass deep to a tall Indian," answers Honker, who is given to theater on the C.B.

"Think we can make it?"

"No way in hell. We're gonna have to get us a Cat out here to plow that road. It's so deep that a grader wouldn't have a chance."

That could take hours. Meanwhile we settle down to catching up on much needed sleep, listening to the head honchoes trade wisecracks on their radios, maybe play a little cards. Everybody's in a pretty good mood now. When just one thing goes wrong it can be frustrating. But when everything goes wrong, the absurdity of the situation makes it a joke. We sit around and figure out what it's costing the company to get us to work. For wages alone it's a couple of hundred bucks an hour. And who knows how to depreciate equipment and figure fuel usage by the hour? Must be at least as much as the wages. And here we are, sitting in a bus playing cards, God knows how many miles from anything that matters, and outside the wind is blowing at twenty-four miles an hour, and it's thirty-four below, and now the 798ers are insisting that the bus driver get a toilet installed in the bus, " 'cause, Jack, it's asking a lot of a man to have to go outside and piss in that kind of weather. You could flat freeze your dick off. And what if you had a hard on and it got frozen that way? Goddamn my old lady would be happier than she's been since on our honeymoon, when it was pretty much the same situation."

And, in the back of the bus an old timer wakes me up to tell me, "Son, this is a hell of a way to build a pipeline."

And Women, Too

There are, in the midst of machismo and male chauvinist pigs, women who work on the pipeline. There aren't very many. As a matter of fact I worked on only one crew that included a woman. She was an oiler on a Becker hammer-drill rig, greasing and oiling the machine that pounded vertical support members into the ground. She was a strong, hard-working woman, used to the rigors of cold weather. She had lived with her husband in a tent outside Fairbanks for two years. All that Marie lacked was confidence; she had almost been convinced during her two weeks on the job that she couldn't do it. There was a sixty-pound iron ring that had to be handled in all sorts of awkward positions— hanging off the rig twenty feet up in the air or leaning off a piece of scaffolding. The men on the crew had assumed that she wasn't big enough to handle it, and she had come to assume that too. But several times I asked her to help me with the driving collar and she did it. Maybe she was a little clumsy with it, but then, so was I. After that she knew she could handle it.

The members of this particular crew—the operator, two other laborers, and myself—thought Marie was doing a pretty fair job. We were impressed enough simply to consider her a part of the crew and leave it at that. The rest of us did our share both of working hard and fucking around, and so did she.

One evening she was given her walking papers. We never saw her again. The crew went to the foreman and wanted to know where Marie was. "Oh, I didn't fire her," he assured us. "I just got her transferred to another crew. I don't like to have a girl on my crew. They aren't strong enough and they hear all sorts of foul language."

"But she was doing her job as well as anyone else," I said. "And she didn't seem at all concerned about foul language."

"Oh, I see," winked the foreman. "So you were getting a little fucking out of her."

All of the stories of the women who have worked on the pipeline are different, but they usually have a lot in common with this one. First of all the men assume that women can't do the work and then they don't give them a chance to show that they can. And as often as not, women are gotten rid of for one reason or another, usually a bad one. One common bad one is that they won't sleep with the foreman.

Before I began to write about women on the pipeline I had scarcely talked to a woman pipeliner. When there are three hundred men and seven women in a camp, the women are constantly harrassed, watched, and sought after. I didn't want to add to their difficulties. But then I realized that I knew only about three Fairbanks women who had worked on the line, and that didn't seem like enough of a cross section. So I started interviewing.

My first interview didn't go well at all. I picked out a cook who for some vague reason, I suspected, might have some interesting things to say. After keeping my eye on her for a while, I finally caught her alone for a moment. I presented my case: I was writing a book about the pipeline and I wanted an interview.

"I'm too busy."

"It won't take too long," I assured her. "I'd like to hear what you have to say about things."

"I'll tell you what I have to say," she said. "I think I've heard every come on that anybody ever invented, and I'm not interested in yours any more than anyone else's."

So much for that interview.

I decided to try a different approach. It was as I had suspected: the women in the camp were definitely gun-shy. Which is understandable after you've been pestered for a few weeks or months by the horniest guys outside the rapists in San Quentin.

For the next attempted interview I brought along a blue notebook and about a hundred and fifty pages of rough draft material that I had written. The woman didn't want to read it, having just finished a ten-hour day, but she was convinced. Nobody would type a hundred and fifty pages just for an unlikely try at a reluctant piece of ass. She was also exceptionally nice.

For the last three years Virginia had lived with her husband and a dog team in a gold rush-vintage log cabin a few miles from the camp. At first the company didn't want to hire her, but because of the local hire policy they had little choice. She and her old man were the only residents within miles and miles, so they seemed good candidates for any jobs that might open up.

At first they offered her a job in the kitchen. She wanted a laborer's job. They said that wasn't woman's work.

"I told them" she said, "that for the last three years I've been running a dog team, chopping firewood, breaking land for a garden, and doing a hell of a lot of other things that aren't 'woman's work.' I spend most of every day outside, even in the winter, and I don't intend to be cooped up inside any damned kitchen. So they let me be a laborer.''

Having the job didn't do much good, since she wasn't allowed to do any work. She could sit around and draw her pay, but they figured she'd swoon or some other godawful girlish thing if they gave her a shovel.

"You know how chivalrous a Texas foreman can be,'' Virginia laughed. ''Chivalrous enough to keep a woman from working and chivalrous enough to fire her for not working if he takes a notion to.

"Well, I putzed around for a couple of weeks, trying to find myself something to do. They'd put me with the camp laborers, and there really wasn't much for anyone to do. But when there was work and I'd try to help, one of the laborers would take my work away from me. You know, 'Here, let me to that, you'll get all dirty.' But one day there was a truck to unload and the foreman was trying to keep me on the sidelines and make conversation. But all of a sudden I just went up, grabbed a sack of cement, and carried it off. You should have seen them. 'Look, that girl can lift a hundred pounds.' I certainly can lift a hundred pounds. I admit that I can't work as hard as some guys, but I can definitely work harder than the ones who won't do anything at all.''

"Why are you working?'' I asked her.

"Same reason as everybody else, I guess—I want the money. I'd like to build a greenhouse, and I want a real birch dogsled. Jim made one last year, but it's a little on the heavy side. We could probably make a better one, but since we're both making so much money, we'll buy one.''

I asked her if she got hassled much by guys.

"Lots,'' she said. ''It's easier when my old man is in camp, because you know how those Texans are. They'll pretty much leave a girl alone if they figure she belongs to a man. But I still get hassled. Guys are always whistling and making various decent and indecent proposals. On my crew the men have pretty much come to accept me, but that's because they're young and a little more used to working with women. But every time a new bunch of laborers joins the crew I have to start all over again. Fortunately the foreman is won over now. He says I'm the best laborer on the crew. Of course, pipeline standards being what they are . . ."

"Right," I said. "You're bound to be the best on the crew if you come back after lunch."

"You got it," laughed Virginia. "Actually, it's a goddamned hassle all the time. I always feel like I'm under surveillance. Everything I do gets talked about. I'd like to wear a scoop neck blouse when it's hot—what I'd really like to do is take off my shirt and get a tan like the men do—but then I know just what kind of shit I'd have to put up with. I definitely have to compromise. And I have to keep my mouth shut a lot.

"But sometimes I turn the tables on them. Like today we got in a fertilizer truck that we had to unload. It was dusty inside the truck, and god knows what kind of chemicals are in that stuff, so I just sort of wandered off and did some more lady-like work. I let the boys do that one. I'm a laborer. I get out of work I don't want to do, just like any other laborer. Just like you!" she said, pointing a finger at me.

After having interviewed Virginia it was easy. She introduced me to other women in the camp, and on those grounds they were less suspicious. There were two different groups of women, I came to find—those who, often reluctantly, had taken jobs in the kitchen or as maids or secretaries, and those who had busted their way into "men's work." I was fortunate during this period to have so many different women to talk to. There were fifteen or so in a camp of six hundred; back in the good old days at the beginning of the construction there weren't any at all, or sometimes one per camp. Women certainly weren't actively recruited, and they were always discouraged. But more and more of them began to take jobs as pressure mounted for local hire and minority hire. Many of the first women who got jobs were Indians or Eskimos, or at least a quarter or an eighth native—enough to qualify. And then at one point women began to claim the right to step to the front of the line as minorities, claiming rightly that women were a minority on the pipeline. At this time there are nearly two thousand women working on the pipeline, of which more than half do "men's work." That's progress, but women still make up only about 10 percent of the work force.

Naturally women couldn't get into skilled jobs, since very few of them had a history of work in the construction industry. Like other Alaskans, they took jobs for which they qualified—as laborers, oilers out of the Operators' Union, bus and truck drivers, and culinary workers, cooks or maids. They also got jobs as secretaries and organizers of recreational activities, and as other clerical workers. It is typical of the oil companies to make sure that clerical jobs were not unionized, so a secretary would often make the astronomical wage of $1600 a month, about as much as a pipewelder grosses a week.

I talked to Liz, a clerk in charge of assigning rooms in the camp. She gave me a whole afternoon, while on duty, and we were constantly interrupted by supervisors, executives, and male clerks from other departments who came up to her window and then claimed to have forgotten what they had wanted to ask about. Liz, who had a B.A. in sociology and had taught school in an Alaska fishing village for a year before going after the big money, gave me more insights into the condition of women on the pipeline than anyone else I talked to. She described herself as "a feminist after my own fashion."

"It is a part of my training to be understanding," she said, "but it gets so damned difficult sometimes. I am constantly patronized, harrassed, and more important but less evident, held down. The job that I do is one that anyone at all could do with a day's training. But there's no hope of my moving into a managerial position. I'm much more educated than the guys who work above me, but I'm sure I'll never be offered a better job. You've got to understand, the men who are running this pipeline are some of the most reactionary in the country. They like their women in skirts—that's why I wear these ratty blue jeans—and they want them to act like little wives. I never hear anyone say "Fuck" unless they forget I'm around, and then they apologize. Everyone is disgustingly nice to me. I am not allowed to see any reality at all. They want to talk to me. Jesus, I can understand that. There are some awfully lonely, horny men around here. But it's hard to put up with all the same. It was worse when there were fewer women."

I asked her how she felt about living among five hundred men who were definitely after her body.

"At first," she said, "I really got a kick out of it. I think many women who come to work feel the same way. All that attention and all those men! It can turn a girl's head! I had to exert extraordinary will power to be moderate—like one man a night. I was blown away by the whole thing. It was really exciting, being 'your complete sex object.' But then I began to realize the cause of all this, and I couldn't live with it anymore."

I told her Brigid Brophy's fable of "The Singularly Ugly Princess." The ugly, despised princess in the story meets a magic toad with a ruby in its forehead and is given one wish. She wishes to become "the most beautiful woman in the kingdom." Immediately there ensues a plague, and all the other women die off. In the end, she is without a doubt the most beautiful woman in the kingdom.

"Yeah, it's something like that," replied Liz. "But what gets to me is being treated like I was sub-human. It's automatically assumed that I can't open doors, and that I don't have the faintest resemblance of a thought in my pretty little head. I'm treated like a child. Sometimes I wish

I wasn't so goddamned understanding about it. It's absolutely absurd that this should be a camp full of *men*. If men worked with women they'd get to know a little more about them and would stop thinking of them as the enemy, something to overcome. It's a completely artificial situation. And I don't like the rumors that are always going around. If I talk to a man it's immediately assumed that I'm sleeping with him. And what if I am? That's my business.''

Apparently it wasn't her business. Later in the summer the twenty-eight women who worked at this camp were gathered into the movie theater and told that V.D. was reaching epidemic proportions in the camp and that they had better stop sleeping around. They were held totally responsible. The men were not given any similar warning. Boys will be boys, but girls had damned well better be nuns.

As I interviewed more and more women I came across the same stories again and again. There were women who seemed perfectly happy with their lot, like a mother-daughter team that was working to save the money to buy a fast-food franchise: "Some girls do it, and some don't," the daughter told me. "If everyone knows you don't, they respect you. I never have any problems." This is apparently the ideal mentality for working on the pipeline. The problem is that it is not a very prevalent one. Being calmly accepting and happy with your lot is just not possible for most of the women.

"I hate men," said a surveyor from Fairbanks. "Not all men, but most of them who work on the pipeline I have come to hate. Every day it's the same old bullshit."

I asked her why that was the case.

"I have been hounded from one end of the pipeline to the other. Since I'm a surveyor, I was on some of the early crews when there weren't any other women in the camps. It didn't matter to me, except I didn't like being away from my old man. But it was weird then. They didn't have any special toilet facilities for women. I'd wander into the john, walk behind the guys at the urinals and go into a stall. They were mortified. Really confused. They were pathetic. They wanted to get rid of me because there weren't any toilets for women.

"And then there was the job. All those full-of-shit macho cowboys trying to impress me with what big men they were. They wouldn't let me do my job, constantly harrassing me. Then the foreman made it clear: either I sleep with him or get fired. He didn't even like me; it was just another macho trip. It seems like either I get fired for not sleeping with the boss, or I get laid off because I'm not working—and I'm not working because they won't let me work. The cards are stacked."

She went through the same thing time and again. There were transfers to other jobs, threats, made-up complaints. She was a hard-liner, and the pipeliners didn't like that.

"I've lived in Alaska a long time, and I know how to survey. I wasn't about to take any shit from Texans who don't even know how to stay warm in the winter. When they hassled me I told them to fuck themselves."

I asked her why she worked on the line.

"In case you haven't noticed," she said, "it takes a lot of money to live in Fairbanks these days. I want to go back to school next winter, so I'm trying to get something saved. But I don't know if I can take it anymore. All those tough strong men building themselves a pipeline in the cold and whining about how much they need a woman. To hell with them! I like being out on the tundra, and surveying is nice because you get to work a long ways from machines, out by yourself. I like being outside, even in the winter, but I don't know how much more I can put up with."

The story of not being allowed to do the work and then getting laid off when it comes time for a reduction in force occurs again and again. When a woman gets hired, the foreman will often take it upon himself to "explain the job to her." Men, of course, are simply put out on the firing line; they presumably know their job. But a woman's first few days at work, unless she's in a kitchen, are spent riding around in the foreman's pickup, fighting off sexual advances and hearing stories about the rigors of the job. I have heard foremen arguing when a new woman is hired: "I get this one. You had the last one."

Finally the woman is put out to work, and then every preconception about women and work that any crew member might have is brought into play. Things are endlessly explained. She has to talk, tell whether she's married, where she grew up. For a man all it takes to do the job is a pair of hands and a desire for large amounts of money; a woman has to give her life history, views on any and every subject, and a resume of past work experience. Chivalry demands that she receive constant offers of cigarettes, pot, shared lunches, and long glances. She must never be allowed to be alone. She is flattered and hears nothing but "clean" language, which means that it is stuttering and disjointed, because normal pipeliner talk includes some form of four-letter word about every fifth word. Women are constantly on trial. They are watched to see if they are doing the job. With men, it is universally admitted that some do the job, some don't. It all pays the same.

But women have to produce. If they slip up, everyone knows it. If they come to work hungover or drugged out or just plain uninterested, as half the men do every day, it is assumed that they must be having their period. They can get away with nothing. There is constant discussion about whether they can do the job or not. If a woman doesn't do the job, even if she is never given a chance to, it is assumed that she can't do it. As the surveyor said, the cards are stacked.

Unless the woman is very special—a hard worker and possessor of such extraordinary social talents that she can somehow appease everyone—she will be "terminated," as the bureaucratese goes. She may be laid off, which is to her advantage, since she can then go to work with the same company again, or she may be fired for some drummed up reason like "personality conflict," which may usually be translated as "unwilling to sleep with the foreman." Or she may be fired simply for not doing the job.

Can women actually do the job? Are they big enough and strong enough to handle most pipeline jobs? From what I have said already about the work, it should be clear that the answer is "usually." Perhaps not every woman could do every job, but that is not the issue. There is really no reason to think in those terms. It is perfectly true that the average woman is smaller and has less physical strength than the average man. But there are small men working on the pipeline, and there are big women who can't get a job, or who are quickly fired with the excuse that they can't do the job. Most of the jobs do not require great physical strength, and strength certainly wasn't the main requirement for most of the jobs I had. It is rarely necessary to lift a hundred pounds, and it's never necessary if you don't want to or can't. I have occasionally hoisted two or three oak skids onto my shoulder and toted them to where they were needed. But no one asked me to do that. I was doing it for fun, for the sheer joy of working hard, or because the laborers were competing to see who could pack the most skids. But my 135-pound, skinny hippie partner wasn't packing three. He carried one and chided me for being too lazy to make the extra trips.

You get the most physical exercise as a laborer. The rest of the trades involve lighter work. It assuredly takes very little strength to drive a truck, especially when it has power steering and an automatic transmission. It definitely takes some training to guide an eighteen wheeler over ice and snow along the treacherous road of the pipeline route. But an Alaska woman who knows winter driving will be better at piloting a bus around the camp, or driving a pickup truck, than a man from California who has never had the experience of an all-out four-wheel skid on an icy road.

And it is the rare pipeliner who works all day long. Women can assuredly handle drinking coffee, smoking cigarettes, and bullshitting as well as the men. I would say that on almost any job I had, almost any woman could have replaced me. The work is simply not that hard. For the most part, if you can handle boredom, cold weather, mosquitoes, and living in a camp, you can handle the job.

There is an unwritten tradition in the trade which shows that the universal prejudice against women is nothing but empty prejudice. The policy is, if you can't do the job, you don't have to. Something else will be found for you to do. This is constantly brought into play with older men. If a sixty-year-old man can't pack buckets of cement, he doesn't have to. That's all there is to it. There are plenty of other jobs. Men on their last legs, who probably ought to be in a hospital, are working on the pipeline. They wave flags at trucks or clean up the shack and make coffee in the morning. And there are men who simply aren't very big. If they can't pack two skids they pack one, and if they can't do that they do something else. Foremen are very understanding: "It's no man's fault if he's a little feller. So long as he wants to work, by god we'll find something for him to do." Men with bad backs are not issued shovels and told to dig. That simply is not the way it's done. If there are tasks which require giants, well, there are plenty of lumbering giants around. And one must remember that even in Alaska we are in the mechanical age. No one is expected to break his back lifting three hundred pounds. That's what forklifts, cranes, and sidebooms are for. Much is made of being able to hold a sixteen-pound sledge hammer straight out in front of you; it's an old construction site competition. But most men can't do it, and those who can't don't feel particularly badly about it. I sure as hell don't. I'm a man, not a weight-lifting machine.

In summary, most jobs don't require any abilities that women don't have or can't learn. It is always more in your favor to have a brother-in-law who is a foreman than to be a hulking muscle man if you're trying to get a job in construction. One of the best sideboom operators I ever saw was only five-foot-three, but wiry. And it is well-documented that although the average woman is much less strong than the average man, as they both approach athletic condition, the gap narrows. In order to learn to work, you need simply to work. Working gets you in shape, and along the way you learn lots of little tricks to make up for lack of physical strength. Learning to use your body weight, to swing loads instead of lifting them, to use your hips and thighs and knees, are all more advantageous than simply weighing two hundred pounds.

It is a shame that women have been discouraged or even systematically excluded from getting jobs on the pipeline. Beyond all the questions of doing the job, the pipeline is simply a free ride for many, many people, and women surely ought to be allowed to cash in on it.

Male pipeline workers see their female counterparts pretty much as they want to see them, and it has little to do with the women themselves, since most of the men have never actually had a conversation with one of them. A handful have worked with one or more women, and so know at least something about it, but the knowledge of most resides in tales they have heard.

There is, of course, a wide spectrum of opinions on women and work, ranging from platitudes such as "A woman's place is in the home" to suspicion, to a desire for available sex, to a wholehearted acceptance of women as workers and equals. In broad terms, the opinions divide along the usual professional pipeliner/pipelining hippie split.

Pipeliners don't know just what to think about women. They definitely do not want to work with women, although for sexual purposes they would like women to be available. But instead of working with them, they would prefer that there be a brothel in each and every camp. I have heard this idea seriously proposed, and a good deal more than once. The pipeliners sit around in the warm-up shacks and argue whether it should be a company run whorehouse or more of a covert operation. They work out the intricate details of V.D. control, rates, and race. The tone of the discussion is the same as if they were considering what magazines they would like to see in the commissary.

There are a multitude of reasons why pipeliners do not want women on the job. One is that it threatens the myth that I spoke of before, the myth of the strong, hard-drinking men who are building the pipeline. If half the crew were women, that would certainly start the myth on its way down the drain. Women destroy the feeling of "being with the boys." God knows what would become of the habitual farting, spitting on the floor, pissing in the snow, and telling stories about the stupidity and sexual appetites of women. "Shit, there'd be fucking mauve curtains in the warm-up shack and you'd have to watch your language. We'd have to throw out the fuckbooks and clean the place up. It just wouldn't be the same."

And then, too, you've got to admit that a girl wouldn't look very *pretty* when she got into a parka and down pants and big old clodhopping boots. "Shit, she'd look as ugly as all them other longhairs."

And then there's another tactic: The work is too hard for women and they can't take the cold. No matter that women can take cold at least as well, if not better, than men. It threatens the myth. And no matter that the job consists of sitting in the warm-up shack six or seven hours a day and then doing a job that any human over the age of twelve is fit to do—it's too hard for women. Might put (God forbid) muscles on them!

There's the employment angle. If women work it takes jobs away from men. Just why a single woman has less right to a high-paying job than a single man is left unclear. And, of course, it's simply assumed that married women wouldn't want to work, or at least shouldn't. But what if they do? Maybe they have husbands who'd like to be supported for a while. Or maybe they prefer to have enough income so they needn't be married at all.

When it comes to sex, pipeliners want it both ways. They want their women pure, and they want them to fuck. Women who don't fuck are roundly denounced as "frigid." Whores are fascinating for their open sexuality but are at the same time the scum of the earth. With this logic in operation, the women in a camp don't have a chance.

There almost certainly have been hookers who got a job, came to a camp, and made a fortune. It at least seems very possible, and I am perfectly willing to believe that there have been a goodly number of them. It would seem an ideal place to be in business. But to hear the warm-up shack conversations, there has never been a woman come to camp who *wasn't* a hooker. The rumors rage.

"I hear that cute little bullcook that just came to camp is selling it!" drawls Clyde.

"That right?" answers Fred. "What's she charging?"

"Hunnert bucks, from what I hear," says Clyde.

"I wouldn't pay no hunnert bucks for that piece of ass," says Fred.

Later in the day it's brought up again: "Say Fred, you gonna fuck that little bullcook? She'd probably do it for fifty, seeing as how it's you."

"I'm thinking about it," answers Fred.

Soon the whole crew is discussing her merits. There is an incredible will to believe that she's selling it, or hopefully, that she's "giving it away." But if she's selling it, that's okay. Pipeliners are all for hookers.

A new fellow on the crew drawls: "I'm what they call a bi-sexual."

Stunned silence.

"What I mean to say," he explains, "is that if I can't get it free, I'll damn sure buy it."

But at the same time the pipeliners hate prostitutes with a vengeance usually reserved for rattlesnakes. They aren't real women, but some sort of mutant, an unnatural species, carrying diseases, ready at any moment to strike down the innocent man just looking for a good time. "Why, I've fucked women that wasn't fit to scrub my wife's floors," says a welder.

The problem, I think, comes down to the fact that pipeliners just don't know many women. They're away from home eight or ten months of the year, and when they are home they go hunting and fishing. There aren't any women working on the job with them, and the only available women are those who will part with their time for a dollar a minute and up. It is easy to continue to believe the myths about women when everyone around you believes them and there aren't any women around to disprove them.

The younger workers are much kinder to women. A man and a woman who come to Alaska together and build a cabin usually build it together. While Alaska is surely not a hotbed of feminism, the vision of the helpless woman tends to break down when women are proving daily that they're not helpless. When it comes to pipelining, since so many of the young workers are not professional construction men, they can understand that a woman might learn the job— after all, they just learned it themselves. The situation with the young workers is—like that of the society at large— some think as their fathers, some simply like women, and some are behind Gloria Steinham all the way. To most it seems clear that the camps would be a lot nicer place to live if there were some women around, and young workers aren't so fascinated by hookers as the old-timers are; they are able to see a lot more in women than fifteen minutes of purchased sex. And besides this, young workers tend to be closer to their feelings than the lifetime construction workers who gave up on their emotional needs a long time back. Living without women makes you desperate for them, makes them strangers, alien, and after a while, the enemy. Having a brothel in every camp doesn't seem much of a solution to this problem, and so out of sheer self-interest many men would be perfectly willing to work with women.

I suppose there will be those who are disappointed that I haven't said anything about whether the women of the pipeline are good looking or not. And I'm not going to. I haven't stacked the men on the scales of beauty, and I'm not going to put the women on them, either. A worker is a worker, and whether you're pretty as the day is long or ugly as a day-old dog—it all pays the same.

Throwing It Away

I once worked for H.C. Price, a major pipeline contractor, at a site outside Fairbanks. The job at that particular place was done, and we were getting set to move, lock, stock, and barrel, to another worksite. Moving the equipment wasn't any problem—the operators just drove it onto the lowboys (low trailers pulled by a conventional tractor, say a Kenworth or a Peterbilt) and we were ready to go. But we had to take the warm-up shack with us too.

Now usually, moving an eight-by-sixteen building isn't very difficult. I have some experience in this sort of work, and if someone were to hire me to move such a building, I'd charge from a hundred to two hundred dollars, depending on how much my employer could afford. There's a sort of standard procedure for doing such a job. While it's best to have two guys to work at it, one can do it. First you dig some holes around the edges so that you can get building jacks under it. When you get it off the ground, you shove some timbers underneath and put the jacks under them.

After a while you have it high enough that a trailer can be backed under the building, then you let your jacks down and you're on your way. I'd figure on the job taking all day; if things went right it could be done in a few hours.

On the pipeline, however, the rule is: if you can bring some equipment into the act, never do it by hand. And if you can use a whole crew instead of just two guys, go right ahead. Full employment for all. So all ten of us set right to work.

Someone came up with a plan. There were a couple of eyebolts screwed into the front of the building, and to these eyebolts were attached stranded steel chokers. The lowboy was backed up to within fifteen feet of the shack, two small trenches were dug under it, and timbers laid from the trenches to the back of the lowboy. At the far end of the lowboy a D-8 Cat hooked on to the cables and started to pull. The shack was supposed to skid up the timbers and come to rest on the trailer.

Everything was rigged up, the operator throttled up his Cat. The foreman gave the go-ahead signal—and the eyebolts ripped out of the wood. They were only sunk in about an inch and a half. We decided it was time for a coffee break.

We drank coffee and tore into plan number two. This time we ran a cable all the way around the building, and the Cat hooked on to that. It started pulling. The cable sank into the sides of the shack, but it started to go up the ramp. Then we noticed it was pulling off to one side. "Son," the foreman said to me, "would you run over and tell a couple of them operators to unload their Cats from the trailers. I got some work for them."

I ran and got the operators while the other three laborers, the foreman, the Cat skinner, and two standby mechanics drank some more coffee. In half an hour we were ready to go again. This time we positioned a D-6 on one side of the shack and a D-8 on the other. They raised their blades and shoved this way and that as the D-8 up front pulled on the cables. Everything inside the shack was getting turned over, and the propane bottles chained to the side were breaking loose from their moorings. We stopped to take them off before there was an explosion, and then it was lunchtime. We hit it again right after lunch.

It wasn't a total loss. The shack, it is true, was somewhat bent out of shape and the door had come off its hinges. But it was on the lowboy. There have been worse jobs. What I would have done for two hundred dollars had only taken ten workers and three Caterpillars six hours to do. Probably didn't cost more than a couple thousand dollars to deliver that shack to it's new location. It's true that it no longer had a door on it, but a couple of carpenters could fix that in no time.

If this were a one-of-a-kind story, I wouldn't have bothered telling it. But it isn't unique. This sort of thing happens all the time, and most anyone who has worked on the pipeline will be glad to tell you a similar story. I always made it a point, when joining a new crew, to ask them to tell me about the biggest fuck-up they had ever gotten involved in.

Several people told me about a hole in the ground, four feet by six feet by two feet deep, that somehow had a total cost of thirty thousand dollars. And all up and down the line there are stories of crews that have simply been forgotten. Once upon a time they had a job to do, but now the job is done. It seems that only the crew understands this, so day after day they go to the same worksite to do nothing. I was a member of such a crew on one occasion. Our job was to unload trucks, but the last truck arrived and was unloaded four days before the word was passed along that there would be no more.

If I didn't know that Alyeska is in the business of pipeline building, I would think that their sole purpose was to spend money. They constantly release statements concerning the amount of money they are spending, breaking it down in various ways so as to be more impressive or understandable. The latest estimate is that the pipeline will cost a total of $7 billion. Or as a newspaper headline read, $5 million a day from now till it's done. Or locally, a million a day in the Fairbanks area. They seem to be extraordinarily proud that they can get rid of that much money that fast.

I have already discussed in some detail the problem of wasted effort, the overabundance of workers and the like. There are good reasons for much of the wasted time—the special circumstances of cold weather, attendant equipment down time, and the simple fact that there is always some wasted time on construction projects—there's just no way to make them as grueling and efficient as production-line operations. But in some large measure, the story of wasted time, money, materials, etc. on the pipeline is a tale of massive ineptitude, poor management and planning, and a "Don't worry there's more money where that came from" attitude. The magnitude of the project, coupled with the cost-plus contract, makes it impossible to control the amount of money being spent, and the whole idea anyway is to spend as much as you can, not as little. This is no cut-rate project.

If we are really to come to terms with the question of waste, we must ask, "Why was this pipeline built in the first place?" And the most obvious answer is that a lot of people stand to make a lot of money from it. There are ten billion barrels of oil in Prudhoe Bay, and the cost of the pipeline is roughly $7 billion. It appears that one could make some money at that rate, and the oil companies are counting on it. One market analyst estimates that the profits, after taxes, will amount to over one billion dollars a year. The Interstate Commerce Commission allows the oil companies to receive a return on investment of only 7 percent per year, but this is 7 percent of the total cost of the project. Ninety percent of the financing of the pipeline was done with borrowed money, and the interest is figured into total cost. The actual return on investment by the oil companies will actually be more like 70 percent. Thus, the pipeline will pay for itself in the first two years of operation, and all the rest is gravy. Now we begin to understand why Alyeska is not worried about a few million dollars here and a few million there. Even an extra billion dollars thrown away is of little note—the important thing is to get that oil to the United States and start counting the money.

But how much oil is ten billion barrels? We are constantly told that it will supply U.S. needs for twenty or thirty years, but that is only a measure of how long it will take to get all that oil down to the lower 48 to be used. In actuality, ten billion barrels of oil would supply total U.S. needs for only about two to three years. Put in those terms there isn't all that much oil in Prudhoe Bay. And when it gets to where it can be used, it will very probably be more expensive than other petroleum, owing to high costs of production.

If the purpose of this oil is defined as making a lot of money for a lot of people, it will do that job—at a cost to the American consumer. But if that oil is meant to supply U.S. energy needs, the pipeline is a waste of money. Seven billion dollars put into the research and development of alternative energy forms would in all likelihood prevent an energy shortage for decades or even centuries to come. I once knew an engineer in Denver who had published a book detailing his plan for building a solar heating plant that could provide total electricity needs for thirty-five Denver homes. The projected cost was $70,000. He couldn't even raise ten thousand. Yet seven billion dollars have been used to get hold of oil that will be used up by the end of the century. We well may wish we had that oil at some future date when oil has become too scarce even to make pharmaceutical supplies, fertilizers, and plastics.

It is, of course, pointless to argue at this time that the Alaska pipeline should never have been built at all. It is nearing completion, and there is certainly no possibility of stopping it. I have included this chapter on waste because I think that the American consumer has a right to know how his or her money is being thrown away. Nor, from what pipeliners have told me about other pipelines, is the Alaska pipeline completely unique in the way that the operation is being carried out. The situation in Alaska is extreme, but I have come to understand that oil companies have always been very liberal when it comes to spending their customers' money.

I once had a job at Old Man camp, a few miles inside the Arctic Circle, and we didn't have a warm-up shack. Instead, on this job the five-man crew stayed warm (I mean "stayed warm" not "got warmed up"—we rarely went outside), inside a forty-eight passenger bus. There was a day crew and a night crew, so the bus ran twenty-four hours a day, using a gallon of gasoline an hour, give or take a little. On our twelve hour shift we were using twelve gallons of gasoline—just to keep warm! And by the time gasoline is gotten to Old Man camp, it is probably worth at least two bucks a gallon. While sitting in this bus, I became enamored of the notion that the pipeline was just a joke, a government job to provide employment for poor Alaskans, and that they were using more fuel to build it than there was in Prudhoe Bay.

It didn't take me long to find out that I was in error. Alyeska has published figures on the subject, and the total projected construction usage is 215 million gallons, plus 3.5 million gallons of jet fuel. That's a far cry from ten billion barrels (at 42 gallons per barrel) but it is a lot of fuel. And I think I can state without stretching the truth that half of that fuel is squandered. A multitude of examples of excessive fuel use immediately come to mind. Trucks are idled all night long for no other reason than so they will be warm in the morning. The camps are not as well insulated as they ought to be, and are often kept at eighty degrees. Equipment sits on the right-of-way and idles for months without being used. It is simply forgotten about, except by the fueler, who fills it up every day.

In mid-winter in Prudhoe Bay I sat inside a warm-up shack that was heated by two fifteen-hundred-watt electric heaters. We also had a coffee pot and a hundred-watt light bulb. At most we needed five thousand watts to keep us warm, and have plenty of light and coffee. Outside the shack sat a fifty-kilowatt diesel generator, using about thirty gallons of fuel a day. We were using four kilowatts, and the other forty-six were just going along for the ride.

I asked the foreman why we had such a big generator.

"Well, son," he began, being from Arkansas and older than me, "last fall we was thinking we might put a circulating engine heater on the crane and plug her in at night, and then we figured we'd need a big generator. But we never got around to that, so we just let the crane idle all night."

The generator idles all night, too. Even though the door on the shack wouldn't close all the way, it was always a steady eighty degrees when we got there in the morning. There's no energy crisis in Prudhoe Bay.

At one point there was an energy crisis, however. The Yukon River froze up, just like it has every winter for the last thousand years or so, but this singular phenomenon took everyone by surprise. This was before the Yukon River bridge was built, when the method had been to ferry supplies across the river while it was open, and then once it got cold, build an ice bridge. There is, however, a period of six weeks or two months in between the last ferry trip and the time the ice bridge is strong enough to take traffic. Since insufficient fuel had been stock-piled, at least one camp, Cold Foot, began to run out of fuel. Something had to be done, so fuel was flown by helicopter, two barrels at a time, across the Yukon River, at a cost of $400 per hour. I never found out what the final tab came to.

The extent to which airplanes and helicopters are needlessly used on the pipeline is truly amazing. It is understandable that, when a piece of equipment is down and parts are needed, they are flown in. It is less understandable that there have been massive airlifts of things like office furniture and lumber. I was in Prudhoe Bay when a load of pipeline skids, four-by-six-inch timbers, about four and a half feet long, arrived in a Hercules cargo plane. And I was at Ft. Wainwright when a load of desks was flown in from Seattle, because "they were needed." This can only represent a lack of management, since there are always trucks running from Fairbanks to Prudhoe Bay, as well as from Seattle to Fairbanks.

Throughout the north, the pipeline builders have become known not only for their waste of fuel, but of any material they can get their hands on. There is waste in any construction job, but it comes nowhere near the magnitude of the waste on this project. In Fairbanks, anyone who wants to be patient and pick through the waste from the pipeyard can get most of the materials it takes to build a house. An inveterate scrounger myself, I have always admired the pipeline dumps for their selection and high quality. Everything you could want is in them, including a number of materials that must surely have been put there because no one could figure out what to do with them.

The pipeline builders thrive on buying things. If there is any need at all for a piece of equipment, it is purchased. In Fairbanks, there are fantastic numbers of yellow pickup trucks. The color, along with the numbers spray-painted on the side, identify them as belonging to Alyeska or one of the subcontractors. A favorite game of Fairbanksans is to count the number of yellow trucks sitting at bars and restaurants. A hitchhiking woman friend tells me she can always count on a ride from a yellow pickup. The driver is most likely not going anywhere in particular, and he's perfectly happy to give a lady a lift, even if she lives ten miles out of town.

The waste of materials in the camps is outrageous. It costs a lot to get something to a camp, but once there, it has very little resale value, since it would also cost a lot to ship it back.

At this point it is even uncertain what will become of the camps themselves when the line is finished. It would definitely cost too much to bring them back to where anyone would want to buy them. They may well be burned— housing for ten or twelve thousand people. It is scarcely credible, but that is the word I get.

It is difficult to speak of the waste on the pipeline because it does not occur in a central location. It is all pervasive. I can point out example after example of needless, senseless waste, waste which in the end is only a matter of transferring money from the pockets of consumers to the coffers of the oil companies. Individually they might be overlooked, but taken together they add up to nothing more nor less than robbery.

I was working on a ditching crew at Prospect Creek. The cables used on the backhoes were of three different lengths: 65, 90, and 115 feet. They broke constantly, often only because the operator got a kick out of seeing them snap. And we constantly replaced them. But if five feet broke off the end of a 115-foot cable, it was not recut and used later as a 90 footer. No indeed, it was left lying beside the right of way, where a clean-up crew would at some later date find employment in hauling it to a dump. And three-quarter-inch stranded steel cable doesn't come cheap. In the lower 48 the price is just under a dollar a foot.

It is not unusual to see all kinds of material simply left lying beside the road. Oak pipeline skids, which cost about $12 each by the time they arrive on the pipeline, are routinely left beside the road or burned. I used to pick them up and burn them in my stove at home. At least someone got some use out of them.

For a while there was much discussion among Alaskans about what would become of all the beautiful new four-wheel-drive vehicles which Alyeska bought for use on the pipeline. At first it was thought that they would be shipped back to the states so as not to put Alaskan car dealers out of business. It is now becoming clear that it doesn't much matter what happens to them. After having been ill-treated for a few years they are virtually worthless. They are constantly getting run into trees, other trucks, and ditches. Their drivers let them idle all night so that they'll be warm in the morning, which is very hard on the engine, and if the truck starts to run badly, the driver may well rev it up and blow the engine, just to be rid of the damned thing. This once proud fleet of four-wheel-drive vehicles is by now the sorriest looking assortment of rusted pieces of bent junk you'd ever want to see. There simply isn't going to be much to get rid of.

Although the waste of food wouldn't seem to amount to much, when there are forty thousand or more meals a day being served, the scraps add up. And food is wasted in enormous quantities. Institutional cooking, of course, lends itself to waste, but on the pipeline it gets out of hand. The prepackaged lunches which are served are a good example. In the morning you pick up a cardboard box full of food. The typical box lunch starts with two sandwiches, one on white bread and one on whole wheat. Most people throw away the white bread and eat whatever is inside. And then there is a piece of fruit, a can of pudding, a bag of potato chips, a can of Vienna sausages, some Hostess Twinkies, a candy bar, and a sealed bag of peanuts. To go along with this meal there are plastic utensils, napkins, and a full range of condiments. On the side you pick up your own soft drinks, milk, coffee, and doughnuts or sweet rolls. The theory is that there should be something for everyone inside the box, though it is unlikely that anyone could or would eat it all. And there assuredly is no man who will eat the plastic and paper. The bus drivers who take the crews to work bring more food and drink. Inside each bus is a garbage can full of soft drinks, milk, and often pastries. If the worksite is in wild territory, and most are, extra food is taken along to feed bears and foxes, which is against policy, but widely practiced all the same.

When the pipeline first kicked off, the food services were on a cost-plus contract too, and then the meals were strictly gourmet. Nothing was too good for the brave men who were building the pipeline. Lobster and frog legs were flown in from Louisiana, and chefs tried their hands at any exotic dishes they imagined would be well received. Cost-plus has since been cut out of the food service end of pipeline building, but pipeline workers still eat better than most people, with steak twice a week and prime rib every Sunday. With reduced costs the price of keeping one man in a camp for a day still runs from fifty to one hundred dollars, or right around half of his wages.

Accusations have been made that Alyeska is being widely ripped off by workers and others, with attendant suggestions that this is what makes the price of the pipeline so high. This is nothing other than P.R. hype, designed to gain public sympathy for the oil companies while representing Alaskans as heartless villains. It is perfectly true that there is theft, but compared to other waste, it amounts to nothing, and furthermore, *no one cares in the least*. When something is stolen, it merely gives the contractor a chance to replace that item with a new one of its kind, and the effect is that he makes more money. If theft were a serious problem, contractors would do something to prevent it, which they don't try to do at all.

For the most part the thievery that occurs on the pipeline is nickle and dime stuff. People simply steal what they need. And because of the waste and the excess of tools and materials, there are few qualms of conscience involved, and even less chance of getting caught. When a worker who is part of a clearing crew notices that the company has sixty new chainsaws, of which twenty are used, he will be very likely to take one if he happens to need it. In most cases the chainsaw won't even be missed, and it is rare that the authorities are even notified.

I have from a friend the story of a Fairbanks man who found a five kilowatt, diesel-powered light plant, an item that almost any Fairbanksan would like to have, since it can provide electricity for your house when the power is out, which is often. The generator was sitting in the road, apparently having come loose from the truck which was towing it. The man hooked on to it and took it home. It had spray-painted numbers on the side which identified it as belonging to a contractor.

For the first day, he couldn't decide whether to keep it or give it back. But on the second day he called the contractor and told him that he'd found one of the contractor's light plants. "But that's impossible," replied the man at the office.

"What do you mean?" asked the man who'd found it.

"Well, it's impossible because we haven't lost one."

So one Fairbanks man has a new five-kilowatt generator. It works fine.

Another example of the ripoff is one which is sometimes practiced by foremen. When a crew member drags up, the foreman will keep him on the payroll, collect his paycheck, and cash it one way or another. Or the terminated employee may split the pay with his boss. Pipeliners claim that this is a very standard and acceptable form of corruption, and has always been the practice on pipelines. They also tell me that foremen who do this almost never go to jail; instead they are reprimanded. I can only assume that if the oil companies were serious about stopping this sort of thing they would stop it. But the fact of the matter is that it doesn't make any difference. There is plenty of money for everyone, and more money if that runs out. The practice is not condoned, but neither is it stopped.

There have been attempts at major, planned ripoffs, but so far as I know none have been succcessful. Two men in a light plane tried to get out of Prudhoe Bay with $130,000 worth of electronic equipment, but they were forced down by technical failure of their plane. The equipment was recovered. While I am not in favor of organized crime stealing Alyeska blind, I would like to point out that $130,000 is not a very serious matter to an outfit that is spending $5 million a day. For publicity purposes it sounds good to reveal this attempted theft, but in reality it is peanuts.

The outrageous waste which is practiced every day on the pipeline encourages theft. Someone who needs something of which the company has an obvious oversupply is not going to think twice about taking it. There has been much furor about "bums" who come sneaking into the Fort Wainwright dining facilities and snap up a free meal. Utter nonsense. Anyone who will throw food away should be willing to give it away, and it isn't as if everyone in Fairbanks is eating at the pipeline dining hall every night, or wants to. The "furor" is strictly for publicity purposes.

The extent to which Alyeska will go for publicity is shown by the pipelaying incident of 1975. CBS crews were on hand to film the laying of the first underground pipe in a northern area of the line. That night the whole wide world saw the pipe and the sidebooms, the ditch and the rigging.

It was impressive. But the world did not see that the next day, the same crews went to work to get that pipe out of the ditch. The pipe should never have gone down in the first place, since there was snow in the ditch, and the extra moisture is not allowable. But the cameras were running. The operation went smoothly. How much did that exercise cost? I don't know total costs, but labor alone probably came to fifty thousand dollars. Who can tell about the cost of housing and feeding a hundred men for two days, providing fuel and maintenance for a dozen sidebooms, a few Caterpillars, a crane or so? Who's going to feel badly about taking advantage of a free meal when things like that are going on?

The theft on the pipeline is properly seen as just another form of waste, tolerated as all other forms of waste are. When you see fuel being idled away and dumped on the ground you don't feel badly about filling your car's tank from the company barrel. Alaskans by and large are a pretty honest bunch—they won't steal from someone that can't afford to be stolen from. But the way that Alyeska wastes fuel, food, materials, and time makes it obvious that they can afford to waste some more. The wastefulness of the entire project invites more waste.

I will admit that I am pretty well hooked into the Puritan work ethic. I believe, deep down, in working hard and giving an honest day's work for an honest day's pay. But my experience on pipeline jobs has made it clear that that is not what is expected of me.

On one job after another I have had little or nothing to do. I once took a job in Happy Valley Camp, working for AIC-Doyon, a Fairbanks outfit. No one could tell me what I'd be doing when I signed up at the office, but that's not so unusual—bad communications between camp and office are the rule. My first morning on the job the foreman told me to "dick around the warehouse and see if you can find something to do." I found very little to do. I restacked some bags of cement and gave a friendly mechanic a hand at pulling an engine out of a truck. That isn't laborer's work, and I could have been busted for it, but what the hell, it was better than nothing. The second morning the foreman told me to "do whatever you did yesterday." I did. That night I was laid off. It seems that the company was pushing its luck to see if it could get away with keeping two more laborers on the payroll. It couldn't. And so I and the man I had come to camp with went back on the same plane.

The situation sometimes gets so completely out of hand that you can not only expect to get paid for not working, but you also can expect to get paid extra if you do work. I once did a ten-day work stint at the pipeyard in Fairbanks, working on one of the pipe cleaning crews. It was fairly steady work, of course, with the usual long coffee breaks, long lunches, and early quitting times. Toward the end of the project it was turned into a high priority job. The foreman decided that an all-nighter would be justified. At six o'clock in the evening we went home for dinner, and then came back at seven-thirty, assured that we would be paid for the hour and a half break. We worked until midnight, though we were so tired by this time we were accomplishing next to nothing. The next day we couldn't get it together to do any work, and so we hid out and slept in the sun until two in the afternoon, when the foreman told us to go home. The paychecks for that week were truly amazing: we had been paid for eighteen hours on the day we worked until midnight, and for twelve hours the next day. A foreman *appreciates* hands who will work for him, and he's usually not unwilling to ice the cake for them.

There are all sorts of ploys that are used to pay a crew for extra hours. I am told that it is common practice in pipeline construction to pay workers double for extra nasty work, like sloshing around in the mud down in the ditches. And the four-hour call-out rule is constantly used to provide the boys with some extra hours. During the testing phase the pipeliners have it made. Although there is little actual work to do, the hands have to be on the job twenty-four hours a day, most of which are spent sleeping in trucks. And it is not impossible at that time to get paid for a twenty-five hour day, if some high priority job can be found to be performed during the lunch hour.

All this must seem completely absurd to someone who is working at a three-dollar-an-hour, forty-hour-a-week job. Now that I'm not working on the pipeline anymore it seems that way to me, too. But it is certainly not the workers who are to blame. The oil companies have so much money that they don't really mind giving it away, especially if it is tax deductible and can buy them other benefits, such as higher petroleum prices. Knowing what I do, I still feel badly about not working when I'm on the job—but not very badly. Presumably the foreman who ices the cake with extra overtime once had a few pangs of conscience about it, too, but he doesn't anymore. That's just the way pipelines are built.

VII

Environmental Impact

The environmental impact of the Alaska pipeline is and has been so great, and the effects of it so diverse, that it is clearly impossible to cover the story completely in a chapter. To go into it in detail would require a book, and a long one at that. But there is another problem involved: it is often next to impossible to find out about the environmental impact of the pipeline. Nowhere except in politics (and it turns out there's a great deal of politics involved here) is there a greater gap between what really happened and what is reported as having happened. As I noted before, Alyeska is at its best when it comes to conducting public relations campaigns. In the matter of environmental impact they are absolute wizards. From the beginning they have had things their way. For the most part, the press has printed what Alyeska wanted the public to hear.*

---

*There has been one notable exception to this case, and his name is Richard A. Fineberg. Fineberg is a Fairbanksan who has reported on the

113

At first glance the question of environmental impact would seem to center around oil spills. And it does. There have already been large oil spills, both reported and unreported. Some have been cleaned up and others have been covered up, either with snow or silence. But there are also other matters involved. The growth of the Fairbanks area from a population of 15,000 to 60,000 has certainly affected the environment. The fact that a road has been built to the North Slope has affected and will affect the environment. And in the future of the pipeline lies a great number of unanswered questions. What happens if the line breaks? What happens if the tankers that carry the oil from Valdez to California spring a leak? What are the chances of sabotage?

For purposes of presenting this unwieldy mass of problems, I have broken it down into three parts. The first part concerns the ecological problems related to the construction of the line. The second part is a discussion of the impact of the line itself, along with the necessary question marks and scenarios. And the third part is about the impact of uncontrolled and unprecedented growth of Alaska cities, and especially Fairbanks, where I lived and did not find it

---

pipeline in *The All-Alaska Weekly, The Daily News-Miner* (Fairbanks), and *The Anchorage Daily News*. And of all those who have reported on the pipeline, he stands alone as a man who had the courage and audacity to try to find out the truth. Fineberg was never willing to accept the press releases handed out by Alyeska, as most other reporters were. The "easy copy" that others printed was to him too easy; he persisted in looking around and most importantly, *talking to the workers*. While others were printing Alyeska's story of a hundred-gallon oil spill at Galbraith Lake, Fineberg was talking to laborers who were cleaning up the 60,000 gallons of heating fuel that were flowing out of the tanks and toward the lake. Time after time Fineberg broke stories of oil spills, scandals, mismanagement, cover-ups and simple bungling. If it had not been for him we would all know a lot less about the environmental problems of the pipeline, and I would surely have a lot less to put into this chapter.

necessary to do any research to find out what pipeline impact was all about.

Just cover it up with snow

When you first look at the tundra of the North Slope, it might seem that there's nothing you could do that would hurt it. As a matter of fact, anything that you do might actually improve it. It's flat, wet, and barren. There's nothing there.

But on second look you begin to see things. As a matter of fact, there *is* something there, and the more you look, the more you see. There are wildflowers. There are little willow trees, still tiny, but a hundred years old. There are voles, and foxes and wolves that eat the voles; more mosquitoes than you ever bargained for. There are birds, and great herds of caribou. And lots of moss.

If one single thing in this region can be said to be most important, it is the moss. The reason is that moss is a very efficient insulator, and if the soil below the moss were ever to thaw out, the Arctic would change completely. The frozen soil, known as permafrost, holds water on top of the ground, and were this not the case, the Arctic would look more like a desert than a swamp. The northern coast gets only about three inches of precipitation a year, and were it not for the permafrost, which is protected by the moss, the Arctic would be the world's coldest desert, instead of supporting the abundant life that it does.

If the moss is disturbed for any reason, the ground below immediately begins to thaw. About ten years ago a company that was exploring in the Arctic found that its supply planes were missing the landing strip, and in order to identify it they carved out their initials with a Caterpillar at one end of the strip. Today those initials are thirty feet deep.

With a project the size of the Alaska pipeline, the potential for destruction of such a delicate ecology as this is tremendous. In fact, environmentalist groups felt that the destructive potential was so great that no pipeline should be built at all. They were not able to convince the courts of this, but they were able to drive hard bargains concerning the manner in which the pipeline should be built.

Thus, the environmental regulations are more stringent than on any pipeline which has ever been built before. Both for the protection of the land and for the protection of the pipeline, it must be this way. There is no chance of simply digging a ditch and throwing the pipe in it; the oil will be coming through the line at 160 degrees, and no matter how effective the insulation used, it would be likely to melt the permafrost. A measure of how critical the situation is exists in the fact that the permafrost, even when the air above is sixty degrees below zero, stays at about thirty-one and a half degrees. It doesn't take much heat to melt it. If the permafrost were to melt, the pipe would simply sink out of sight.

For this reason great care is taken not to melt the permafrost. Wherever any equipment is operating, it must be done on a five-foot-thick gravel pad; five feet of gravel being equal in insulative value to the original eight or ten inches of moss. If any tundra is accidentally torn up, the area must be reseeded so that the ground is insulated. Through permafrost areas, the pipe is set above ground on vertical support members (VSMs), and thermal heat exchangers, or heat pipes, are installed, which transfer potentially dangerous heat out of the ground. With the environmentalists supplying both pressure and assistance, the situation has been very carefully studied, and the project is for the most part being done with great care.

The control, however, is not perfect. Pipeliners, conservative in all other matters, are equally conservative in this one, and not living in Alaska anyway, they have very little concern for its ecology. And so we do have occasional rowdies riding across the tundra on Caterpillars for the hell of it. Pipeliners *resent* not being allowed to drive across the tundra. They also resent having to hand clear the last hundred feet of pipeline right-of-way before a stream, and on more than one occasion have pushed trees and dirt into a creek. As one of them explained to me, "Shit, everybody knows catfish bite best when the water's roily." There are, by the way, no catfish in Alaska.

And then there are little incidents with the VSMs. Depending on the stability of the soil, the VSM has to go down to a certain depth. In the case that I saw, it was eighteen feet, but the drill crew had made a mistake and the hole was only fifteen feet deep. Call the driller back? No way. The mechanic got out his torch and cut three feet off the pipe, the extra chunk then being buried in the snow before the inspector came around. I don't know how often this is done. I seriously doubt that this was the only time it has happened. Nor do I know whether it will ultimately make any difference. Perhaps the line is being overbuilt by a big enough margin to make things like this unimportant. Of course, it may not be.

And now we come to the matter of oil spills. The single most worrisome thing about the pipeline is that there will be an oil spill. Alyeska says there's no problem, it's all under control. But since construction began, there have been numerous oil spills, and worse than that there have been attempted and successful cover ups of these spills.

Everyone who goes to work on the pipeline is told in orientation that he must report any and every oil spill which he observes, even if it is only one quart of thirty-weight oil. And every employee has it explained to him that he will be in no danger of being fired because of this report. In turn, Alyeska is required to pass the information along to the

Department of Environmental Conservation. A report of any spill larger than twenty gallons is supposed to be given to the press. The purpose of these regulations is to make Alyeska accountable both to the appropriate state agencies and to the public. That is the official policy. The reality is quite another thing.

There have been big oil spills and little oil spills. Oil spills occur constantly. And probably the majority of them have never been reported. There are many factors at work to keep oil spills from being cleaned up and reported, but it is generally the case that Alyeska covers up the big ones and the workers cover up the little ones, sometimes because they are in fear of their jobs if they do report the spills. Oil spills are a pain in the ass for everyone. The fact that a one-quart oil spill must be reported seems merely silly to some. Of course there is no denying that five thousand one-quart spills are equal to 1,250 gallons of oil on the ground.

No one likes to report oil spills. If a laborer reports it, he's the most likely candidate for cleaning it up. And the foreman doesn't want to do any more paperwork than necessary. To pipeliners, of course, oil spills are of no concern whatsoever. They consider the reporting procedures to be a matter of some knee-jerk liberal environmentalist assholes trying to tell them how to do their job. It's a personal insult. I was once threatened that I would be run over with a Cat if I was caught again cleaning up oil on the right-of-way. That is standard. I wasn't singled out for any special hostility; it's just that small oil spills are covered up and forgotten about.

Many workers claim that they have been threatened with being fired if they try to do anything about oil spills. This is easy to believe, especially since some of those who have been so threatened are friends of mine. Redneck foremen don't go for ecology and all that bullshit. Back home they dump as much oil on the ground as they feel like, and that's the way they want to do it in Alaska, too. To them, worrying about the environment is the same thing as worrying about the rights of Communists. Liberal stuff. "We're here to build a pipeline, by God, not worry about goddamn fishes and birds." And so, for one reason or another oil spills are not reported and are not cleaned up.

That is also the case with big oil spills. I made it a point of casually asking my fellow workers about any oil spills they had seen. Almost everyone could tell me about five gallons of oil or fuel that they had seen dumped and never cleaned up. One man told me about two fifty-five gallon drums of fuel that were dropped two hundred feet from a helicopter and promptly forgotten about. Another man told me of a thousand gallons of diesel that was dumped at Dietrich and never reported. Richard Fineberg from time to time has written about oil spills that were not reported, and in a June 27, 1975 story in the *All-Alaska Weekly* he tells of an ironic reversal. It seems that a pipeline official felt that his camp's credibility was threatened by having reported so few oil spills—so he reportedly told a worker to dump some oil on the ground and tell the DEC about it! On the evidence it is safe to assume that over-zealousness in reporting oil spills is not a major problem.

So far as I know, there have thus far been four major, serious oil spills during the construction of the pipeline. Two of them involved cover ups and one was controversial because Alyeska didn't want to clean up the mess when a tanker overturned near Chandalar, dumping 8500 gallons. They claimed it was the responsibility of the trucking company. Again, in three of the cases, it was the ever vigilant Richard Fineberg who broke the story.

The first big leak was at Galbraith Lake. Over an undetermined period of time, an estimated sixty thousand gallons of fuel leaked from an underground pipeline, seeped through the gravel pad on which the camp was built, and began to make its way to the nearby lake. The leak wasn't noticed because the holding tanks were simply filled on a regular schedule, and no one ever kept track of the amount of fuel it took to fill the tanks.

From the beginning it was clear that Alyeska wasn't going to come clean about the spill. At first they insisted that a hundred gallons was all that had been dumped. They denied all reports of amounts larger than that. Then they took the tack that no one really knew how much had been spilled, and that it would be "premature" of them to release an estimate. They mounted an all-out attack on Fineberg for his reporting efforts. They denied that any oil had gotten into a creek which leads to the lake. Then they began to tell of their commendable and far-reaching efforts to keep oil from flowing into the lake. Fineberg reported that there was an oil sheen on the lake. Alyeska denied this. A friend of mine happened to be working at Galbraith Lake at the time, and he told me that not only did oil get into the lake, but the early efforts of the crew he was working with did nothing to stop more oil from flowing into the lake. Many people who were working there at the time were fired for one reason or another in an apparent effort to discredit their testimony. My friend was one of the few who managed to stay on the job.

There was another incident at Isabel Pass in which an explosion went awry in a yard full of barrels of fuel—they were crushed by falling rock. Instead of making any effort to clean up the mess, crews were immediately put on seventeen-hour shifts to try to cover it up. Reason? There was to be an environmental inspection in a couple of days. It was a weekend of frenzied action that showed no concern for anything other than covering up the evidence. Not only was the fuel spilled by the explosion not cleaned up, but oil that was still inside ruptured, half-full drums was dumped onto the ground. They brought in fresh dirt to cover the mess with. Workers who protested were fired. When the environmental inspectors came around on Monday morning they saw a clean, carefully graded surface, with no evidence that there had been a catastrophe a couple of days before. Members of the touring Arctic Environmental Council wanted to stay and talk to the workers, and the workers most certainly wanted to talk to them, but unfortunately there was no time allotted for that.

Another major spill occurred at Prudhoe Bay in January of 1976, this one about seventy thousand gallons. So far as I can determine, there was an all-out effort to clean it up, even though at this time the camps were empty of most of their workers, as they pretty well shut down from December 15 to January 15. It all began when the tanks were topped off at fifty below zero, during a long cold snap. Unpredictably, although it happens all the time, the temperature rose 60 degrees in twelve hours, from fifty below to ten above. The fuel expanded, broke a valve, and spilled on the tundra before anyone knew what had happened. It was one of those things. Officials blamed it on the weather, but the real cause was not the weather, but a *lack of understanding* of the weather. Anyone who has worked in Prudhoe Bay knows that such a temperature rise is possible, but what you've got to do is count on it. This is a very good example of the kind of thing that could so easily go wrong with the pipeline—there are just too many factors to take into consideration, just too many things that nobody thought of.

Although the oil spills and their attendant cover ups have posed the most dramatic examples of environmental damage during the construction of the pipeline, there have been other issues. Sewage disposal has been one of them. Naturally, at each of the camps which Alyeska built, a sewage treatment plant had to be installed. Some of them had to be quite sophisticated, because permafrost affords very poor drainage. It is a problem that anyone who builds anything in Alaska has to cope with. Alyeska, however, didn't want to cope with it. From the beginning they argued that since substandard sewage disposal systems operate in Alaska, theirs should be allowed to be substandard too. As usual, it was Richard Fineberg who covered the story.

There were problems from the beginning. Several sewage treatment plants were inadequate owing to camp populations that were higher than projected, and others simply didn't work. So far as Alyeska was concerned that wasn't important. In early 1975 there were two camps—Galbraith and Five Mile—where camp population was increased while the sewage disposal systems were inadequate to handle even the people that were there. Alyeska had plans to upgrade the systems, but in the meanwhile, said a pipeline official, "We've got to get as many people into the camps as we can." It was strictly full speed ahead, business as usual, and so what if a little sewage is getting into the creeks? A Department of Environmental Conservation official that refused to play ball with Alyeska was fired on trumped up charges of being "uncooperative." He'd been talking to the press about the problems. In the end the problems were solved by a method that one comes to expect from Alyeska—they managed to get legislation pushed through the Alaska government that exempted them from the laws that other Alaskans have to comply with. Par for the course.

There have been other issues, such as tearing up tundra, running equipment into stream beds, and in one case, the unauthorized dynamiting of a river bed to facilitate a pipe crossing. You can't stop a seven-billion-dollar project for a few thousand greyling, as we all know. In general, Alyeska's method has been to do exactly what they want to do.

In some cases they get caught, and in others they don't. But even if they do, it is not likely that they will lose very much. For an outfit that is spending five million dollars a day, a million dollar fine, which is very unlikely to be levied anyway, does not amount to much.

Another big problem related to the construction of the line has been safety. The Elliot Highway, running from a few miles north of Fairbanks to Livengood, has proven to be an extraordinarily dangerous route. It was originally built during the gold rush days and is a poor road by any standards. Tourists used to regard it as something of a challenge. But then some of the biggest trucks in the world began to use it. A pipe-hauling truck when loaded is 100 feet long and ninety thousand pounds—a rig that would be allowed on almost no highway in the United States. And yet they run, at a rate of two hundred a day, over a road that in many places lets two of them pass with only a few millimeters in between, and whose entire length consists of steep grades and sharp turns. The trailers upon which the pipe sits were another subject of controversy. The pipe is hauled in eighty-foot lengths (it could have been hauled in forty-foot lengths). To accommodate three lengths of pipe, special trailers were manufactured, utilizing a self-steering rear axle.

The drivers who risk their lives in these rigs have nothing but complaints. Haul operations were once shut down for several days when the fifth-wheel assemblies, the point at which the trailer hooks onto the tractor, developed cracks in the metal. The self-steering rear axle, which was chosen over the conventional cable-linkage logging truck model, proved to be troublesome. If for some reason the brakes went haywire, and they often did, the trailer had a tendency to pull the whole rig off the road. During one winter month the Highway Department pulled seventy stranded trucks out of the ditch. The truckers refer to the road as the

"Kamikaze Trail." There have been many fatalities. Alyeska could have improved the situation in many ways—by upgrading the road, slowing down the traffic, or hauling pipe in forty-foot lengths—but Alyeska is in the business of building pipelines, not worrying about truck drivers. They routinely blame the large number of accidents on the truck drivers who are inexperienced at driving on ice and snow, ignoring the fact that it was Alyeska who imported them from Texas, and Alyeska who gave them no training.

Even with what Alyeska likes to refer to as "the most stringent environmental regulations outside the nuclear power industry," there has been continual ecological damage caused by the construction of the pipeline. There has been pollution in Prudhoe Bay (which is beautiful in a way, looking like ice cliffs rising half a mile high), hills stripped for the gravel they contained, and a general tearing up of the countryside. In usual corporate fashion, the timber that was knocked down along the pipeline right-of-way was usually burned before anyone could get at it for firewood or cabin logs. Control of Alyeska's activities has been difficult, owing both to the size of the project and the fact that it is strung out along eight hundred miles of territory, making it inaccessible to anyone that Alyeska does not want to give access to; for the press, whirlwind tours have been the order of the day. Nor has Alyeska been overly cooperative with the government monitors who are supposed to be overseeing the construction.

The fact that the pipeline is something less than a total fiasco is due to the efforts of the much maligned environmentalists. Alyeska certainly cares no more about ecology (for all their public relations efforts) than they do about wasted time, money, or materials. Alyeska is ecologically concerned exactly to the extent that it is forced to be. We have the environmentalists to thank for making the pipeline construction less of a mess than it might have been.

The Longest Tube of Chapstick Ever Seen

I've sat in the back of the bus and talked with so many guys about how to blow this line up as soon as it's done. Some have very sophisticated plans. It's hard to tell which ones were just bullshitting and which are stockpiling dynamite, which is easy enough to steal, you know.

A laborer

It is impossible to predict exactly what environmental effects the pipeline will have in the future. The scariest thing would be a break in the line, causing a major oil spill, and the 1972 environmental impact statement allowed that a break during the life of the pipeline is probable. Another problem comes in the transportation of oil from Valdez to California, or Japan, or wherever it eventually ends up. Many ships have cracked up while navigating the coastal waters, and the possibility of it happening again can't be ruled out. There could for one reason or another be a break in the line, and although there are shutoff valves in it, a huge quantity of crude oil would flow out onto the ground, perhaps into rivers and streams, before it could be stopped.

Before we look at the safety features and possible problems of the pipeline, there is another problem that has less obvious immediate impact on the environment. The pipeline has opened up a whole new territory. You can now drive a car from Fairbanks to Prudhoe Bay. Right now there is a major controversy about whether this new road will be opened to the public or not, the environmentally concerned wanting it to remain closed, and those who stand to make some money from it wanting it opened up. In addition to the possible tourist industry, there has been a rash of new exploration in heretofore inaccessible places, and rich copper deposits have been located in the Brooks Range.

In terms of area, the pipeline is only a tiny line on a map of Alaska. The right-of-way is in fact only a hundred feet wide, and so very little land has been disturbed. But it is the access which it provides that is important. Not only people and their cars would travel up the line, but people with their guns, boats, snow machines, swamp buggies, motels, McDonald's hamburger shops, and God knows what else.

It would almost surely become a favorite place for hunting, since the ever-increasing population has significantly depleted the supply of game in areas that are now accessible. The North Slope is full of caribou, which over the past hundred years have become increasingly scarce. Whole herds have been wiped out already, and caribou seem to be an easily spooked animal. After a couple of years of slaughter on the Taylor Highway, which leads to the town of Eagle and then on to Dawson City, Yukon, the main herd simply stopped coming that way. The North Slope may well be their last stand. I would hate to see those beautiful creatures wiped out, and I'd hate to see natives and other homesteaders deprived of one of their major sources of food. But the road may well be opened, because it is the people with money who want it opened. The people who depend on the caribou usually haven't got the price of a can of beans on them.

And, of course, the pipeline opens up the way for more pipelines. Right now there are plans being made for a natural gas line, which may or may not follow the route of the oil line. It may cross entirely new territory, thus opening up more previously undisturbed land, and it is almost certain that it will be built in the same outrageous manner that the first one was.

And now we come to the question of oil spills, which in reality is the question of the pipeline construction's integrity. If something was overlooked by the engineers, if the cumulative result of poor work is serious, if quality control has not been what it was supposed to be, if the line is sabotaged, if it really won't withstand a severe earthquake—then oil will spill. First of all, let us consider what kind of spill we are talking about. Recently there has been some discussion of this issue in the newspapers, and it appears that the matter is a very serious one.

Mechanics Research Inc. (which works for the federal pipeline monitoring agency) in 1974 released an analysis indicating that the best leak detection system Alyeska can come up with will not detect a low-rate leak. And what is a "low-rate leak"? One that is less than 1700 barrels, or 71,400 gallons, in a twenty-four hour period. That's at a flow rate of 1.2 million barrels a day, the projected flow for 1978. Alyeska naturally has challenged this analysis, saying that it is inaccurate and irrelevant, but failed to point out exactly where the error is. Nor do they give an estimate of what the leak detection system will spot, other than to say that at a flow rate of 600,000 barrels a day, it can detect a leak of 744 barrels. Since the plan is to put 1.2 million barrels a day through the line, that estimate sounds completely irrelevant.

The problem with the metering system is that it depends on monitoring the line-volume balance, and as beginning chemistry students learn, in a closed system, volume, pressure, and temperature are all interrelated. There is also the matter of meter accuracy—when you're measuring a volume of 1.2 million barrels, an error of plus or minus one-tenth of 1 percent equals a lot of crude oil. And that is the best that the meters can do. That is *predictable* error.

If the system does detect a leak of more than 1700 barrels per day, operations will begin to shut down within ten seconds. But enormous amounts of oil could spill before the leak was found and repaired. There are sixty block valves on the line, but in one place it is twenty miles between valves. And how much crude will fit into twenty miles of pipe? 132,000 barrels. I don't know what 132,000 barrels of crude oil floating down the Yukon River would look like, but I'd hate to be a salmon if it happened.

Of course, in addition to the computerized leak detection systems, there will be aerial and ground patrols looking for evidence of leaks. But the aerial operations will go on only during the first thirty days of operation, and the weather has to be right. Airplanes spend a lot of time on the ground in Alaska. Minus sixty degree cold, fifty mile an hour wind, fog, and blowing snow constantly keep planes on the ground. As for the ground patrols, there is evidence that it might take an underground leak (and nearly four hundred miles of the line is underground) several weeks to surface. At Galbraith Lake as much as a hundred thousand gallons leaked unnoticed underground while hundreds of workers were walking right over the pipe. And from my work experience I can easily imagine what it will be like to work on the ground patrol. Oh, what a job! Getting high and cruising up and down the pipeline (maybe on snow machines!), looking for leaks that you probably couldn't see anyway. Those who work on the patrol won't be any more conscientious than any other workers. A very laid back job.

In summary, the situation with oil spills is this: there will in all likelihood be one or more breaks in the line, and huge, unimaginable amounts of oil will be dumped. It appears that there is no way to be sure that it won't happen. Alyeska would like to say that a spill is impossible, but not even they have the audacity to say that. All they can say is that they are doing the best that they can, which is probably not true, but it has an aura of credibility about it. In any event, their best has already produced some major oil spills, and it is reasonable to assume it will produce some more.

In 1975 there was a scandal that threatened the integrity of the whole operation. It was immortalized by Richard Fineberg in an article (*All-Alaska Weekly*, 10/24/75), entitled: "X-ray Faking—A Latter-day Alaskan Mellerdrama." As I have noted before, all the welds on the pipeline are required to be X-rayed in order to assure their quality. But X-raying pipe isn't very much fun, especially when it's hot and the mosquitoes are zapping you and you're putting in hundred-hour-plus weeks to stay close to the welders and the equipment (naturally) doesn't work and the foreman is pushing and it all begins to seem a bit on the absurd side. All these problems were suddenly solved in one fell swoop. Someone rather high up in the quality control organization suggested that the technicians find one good weld and X-ray it several times with different identification numbers attached to the X-rays. The word was passed along, and that was exactly what was done.

The sham all came to an end when somebody talked. Alyeska was appropriately embarrassed and ordered an immediate investigation. Many workers resigned, were fired, or were shuffled to other jobs. Ketchbaw, the company whose employees had faked the X-rays, was fired and replaced with another. Corrections were made.

But what started as a three-act "mellerdrama" turned into an epic. Alyeska, after firing Ketchbaw, began a lawsuit against them. Ketchbaw filed a countersuit. A Ketchbaw man in charge of the weld falsifications investigation was found dead in his apartment. One day after his death was pronounced a suicide by the coroner's jury, X-rays of 358 welds were ripped off from an office at the Delta pipeline camp. And eventually, pipe burial was halted for four days by the Department of the Interior. Seems there was a lot of pipe going into the ground without the welds being certified first. A lot of pipe is going to have to be uncovered and X-rayed. Once again, the price of the pipeline is going up. At this time, it appears that the quality control system is at least a total mess, if not simply corrupt. Alyeska has proven beyond a shadow of a doubt that it can't be trusted, and apparently will get some much needed supervision from here on out.

In addition to the outright scandals, there have been numerous other small problems which put the quality of the line in jeopardy. For a good while the placement of the vertical support members caused problems. After being put into the ground, the VSMs were corrugated to improve their bond with the permafrost, and they persisted in cracking. Incredible amounts of time were wasted while engineers tried to figure out the problem. Besides the difficulty with the corrugating machine, which was finally solved, the installation of VSMs has generally been problematic. Once again, the problem is quality control. I worked on a VSM crew for a few weeks, and can verify that it's a haphazard, hit and miss operation. On each crew there is a field geologist, who in actuality has a large amount of responsibility. There is no absolute standard either for the size of pipe to be used or the depth to which the pipe is installed. On the basis of the information he can gather from a hasty analysis of the dirt that comes out of the hole, the "dirt squeezer" must decide the pipe size and hole depth. In some places we would hit gravel or bedrock at thirty feet, thereby giving the VSM a solid base. In other cases the pipe would sink into mush at thirty-five feet, and all the geologist could do was to note that this occurred. Presumably a crew would come along later, weld another piece of pipe to the top of the one that we had started, and drive it in. But as a long-time member of the crew said, "You know them boys that are following us are gonna call it good enough." And I can easily believe that that is the case. Many such problems are solved by the pipeline dictum: "Good enough for who it's for."

All this does not show that a break in the line and consequent oil spill is inevitable, but it does point out a grave possibility. The pipeline has certainly been engineered with great care, and the quality control is superior to, say, a subdivision project. But the question remains: Is it good enough? And no one can answer that question definitively.

Yet, if it isn't good enough, there are extraordinarily serious consequences. There are many, many contingencies which have been considered. I was very impressed, while working on the bent-setting crew, that each day the engineers gave us a figure telling how long our hundred-foot steel tape measures would actually be at thirty, forty, or fifty below zero. Steel contracts as the temperature decreases (at the rate of 6.3 times 10 to the minus 6th per unit per degree F. temperature change), but this is the sort of thing you normally wouldn't think about. When the VSMs have to be set on the button you'd better think about it, however. The danger lurks in what has not been considered. And no one knows what that is.

The line is designed to be earthquake proof. By setting it above ground and insulating the pipe, the possibility of melting the permafrost that holds it up is eliminated. Thermal expansion has been taken care of by putting small bends into the pipe along its whole distance. In this way the pipe will be able to expand and contract at the bends, at the same time sliding on its supports, so that heat will not make the total length any greater, nor cold any shorter. If the pipe were straight it could "grow" nearly half a mile when the temperature increased by a hundred degrees.

For the moment, let us assume that the engineering has been perfect, that absolutely everything has been considered and accounted for, and that the construction, if not perfect, is at least compensated for by the overkill in engineering. In that case there would be no breaks in the line due to defective welds, no problem with earthquakes or temperature gradients, and no cause for alarm over the limited powers of the leak detection system. It would seem we are out of the woods. The pipeline is a billion dollar picnic.

But then there is the problem of sabotage.

There has already been minor sabotage on the line—a piece of pipe rolled off its blocks here, a few hoses cut there, a few hundred pipe X-rays stolen at Delta. There may well be some more serious attempts at sabotage.

The army is prepared for an all-out invasion. Already there have been war games played along a route simulating that of the pipeline. The condition of such an operation would be an all out attack by the Arabs or the Russians or some foreign power. In that case Fort Wainwright, Fort Greeley, and Fort Richardson would all be mobilized and ready to go.

The event of such an attack, however, is highly unlikely. What we should worry about more is a guy with a high-powered rifle and a handful of armor-piercing bullets using the line for target practice. That is the real problem, and one that not much can be done about.

If the eight-hundred-mile pipeline were to be really safe, it would require a security force of perhaps three thousand guards, say one every quarter mile along its route, and also continual aircraft surveillance of the area on both sides of it. That would stop the Sunday shooter. It might not stop a team of men who knew the bush and were interested in getting down to some serious guerilla warfare.

To some I might seem overconcerned with the problem of sabotage, or even downright paranoid. But that is not the case. I am from Alaska, and I know that there are a lot of people who were hurt by the pipeline. I know that there are a lot of people who never wanted it to be built in the first place, and who vowed that if it ever were built they would do their best to shut it down. And Alaskans must represent the most heavily armed populace in the United States. It would not surprise me greatly to learn that there are people who are laying in ammunition and caches of explosives with the intent of shutting the pipeline down before the oil starts to flow.

The sort of people the authorities need to be concerned about are not environmentalists. It would seem rather odd for someone who was concerned about the ecology to cause a major oil spill. But there are others who feel that the pipeline represents an invasion by outsiders, who feel that a state of war has existed between Alyeska and Alaska for the last several years—and Alyeska has been winning. But when the line has oil in it, one man with a stick of dynamite could conceivably shut the line down for months if he were somehow able to cause the oil to stop flowing for a few days at fifty below.

The president of Alyeska discussed this possibility in an interview. The oil is pushed through the line at 160 degrees, heated both by natural gas at the pump stations and by the friction which is created as it travels through the pipe. He admitted that if the line were shut down during the winter, and the oil allowed to cool, that it would form "the longest tube of chapstick ever seen." About the possibility of someone punching holes in the pipe with armor-piercing bullets, he admitted that it could be done, but seemed to take solace in the speculation that with the pressure of the oil coming out through the hole, the shooter could well be killed. Which makes one wonder if standing behind a tree wouldn't be wisest.

It is probably difficult for anyone unfamiliar with Alaska to understand why there should be Alaskans who hate Alyeska and its pipeline so much that they would vow to shut it down. But there are things about the pipeline that bring out such strong emotions in Alaskans.

> *I'm movin' out. Fairbanks ain't a fit place*
> *to live any longer*

There's nothing wrong with Fairbanks that a 50 percent reduction in population wouldn't cure. For Fairbanks, as well as a number of other cities and towns, the problem is nothing other than an old-fashioned population explosion. Too many people, too fast. And they all came to work on the pipeline.

Not everyone agrees that all these extra people are a bad thing. The shopkeepers don't think so. Neither do the land developers, the bankers, the bar owners, or the hookers. All these new people in town have stirred up a hornet's nest of business, and if you want to make a million bucks quick and then split, Alaska is certainly the place to do it.

Of course it's a hell of a place to live in the meantime. It's virtually impossible to make a phone call, and there are lists several months long of new applicants for phone service. Your electricity is likely to go off at any time, and the power companies routinely have to borrow fuel from Alyeska or the army. The power companies themselves have suggested that customers buy portable generators to supply their needs when the power goes out. Heating fuel has been getting more expensive and less abundant all the time. And the latest problem seems to be a water shortage. Of course, if you live outside the city limits, which by now have shrunk to include only a small portion of the actual city, you can't get city water anyway. So if you live on one of those cheap lots ($3,000 an acre), several miles out of town, you can drill a well, often 200 or more feet deep, at a price of $22 a foot.

There is almost no part of life in Fairbanks that is untainted by the presence of Alyeska and its pipeline. Every place of business in the city is busy—so busy that you can count on half an hour's wait at the banks, the post office, the supermarkets, or the lumber yards. And almost anything you could want to buy has been in short supply at one time or another.

The influx of people has caused an unparalleled housing shortage. If you are looking for a place to rent, at any given time you may have a choice of two apartments—a one-bedroom for four-hundred-fifty a month and a two-bedroom for five-fifty. A cabin without plumbing or electricity can be rented for two hundred a month. Likewise, a bed in a dormitory can be had for fifty dollars a week. For the most part there simply isn't anything to rent.

And if you're looking into buying a house you'd better be making pipeline wages. There are no bargains. A no frills twenty-thousand-dollar house will sell for fifty thousand dollars, and it is likely to be so inaccessible that you'll need a four-wheel-drive vehicle to get to it in the winter. Trailer parks, those ubiquitous signs of substandard civilization, have proliferated, since you can still get a two-bedroom model for around thirty thousand dollars. There are endless numbers of people who have simply given up and are living in travel trailers or campers on the back of pickup trucks. If the problem is grim, so is the solution—slapped together ticky-tacky houses and more trailer courts.

But those who are profiting off the ever-increasing population, those who sell things to people, don't have it made either. For it is becoming more and more impossible to maintain a decent standard of living on anything less than pipeline wages. Even with the massive unemployment in Alaska, shopkeepers and restaurant owners find no takers when they advertise jobs for four to six dollars an hour. Or if someone is desperately in need of a job, he may take one of the low-paying jobs for a month or two while his number works its way up on the union list. And then it's off to the Slope. Almost every area is affected by this problem. You can make more money as a pipeline security guard than you can as a city cop or a highway patrolman. You can make more money on the pipeline than you can as a fireman. Teachers can do better for themselves as laborers than they can as teachers.

When Alyeska started hiring, people started quitting their jobs. New people, just come to town to get pipeline jobs, were forced into the jobs the pipeliners had vacated. Then these new people too got pipeline jobs, and more new people took the town jobs. And on and on. It's hard to get a decent meal at a Fairbanks restaurant—all the cooks have gone to the Slope. Bank tellers for the most part have been on the job about three months. Anyone with a job paying less than ten dollars an hour is going to seriously consider going to the Slope. It's a virtual necessity.

Aside from the seemingly natural or at least very American desire to make as much money as possible, as quickly as possible, it seems that everything conspires to make you want to go to work on the pipeline. The cost of living in Fairbanks is so high that you simply can't get by on "reasonable" wages. The case of a Fairbanks family that I know makes this clear. Eric is a skilled diesel mechanic, and he makes a little over ten dollars an hour for a forty hour week. That's twenty thousand a year. His wife makes another seven thousand as a secretary. They live with their four children in a modest-bordering-on-shabby three-bedroom house, which they bought before the pipeline hit, and so have relatively low mortgage payments. They live as moderately as they are able. Eric keeps the family car running. Karen bakes bread and gives the kids homemade birthday presents. But they can't make ends meet, even on twenty-seven thousand dollars a year, which should put them right in there with the upper middle class.

First of all there are income taxes. Even though the cost of living is higher in Alaska than it is anywhere else, taxes are the same for everyone. And in Fairbanks there is a 5 percent sales tax on everything. During the winter it takes a hundred dollars a month for Eric and Karen to heat their home, and it would cost a hundred and fifty if they didn't supplement their oil burning furnace with a woodstove. It costs a dollar a night to keep the circulating heater on the car plugged in during the winter. Food is about 1½ times as expensive as in any place in the lower 48. And as for entertainment, you've got to be a pipeliner to afford that. Any place that has live music, and most of them do, has a two-dollar cover charge. Beer is a buck and a half, a mixed drink a dollar seventy-five. Thus, making twenty thousand a year, Eric is flirting with a poverty line existence. He's always hunting up odd jobs for the weekends, and he's always thinking about leaving the family behind and going to the Slope.

While the average personal income in Alaska has skyrocketed, the quality of life has gone down. No matter how much money you make, there is nothing you can do about the facts of overcrowding, traffic jams, the soaring crime rate, and pollution. If you work on the pipeline you can keep ahead of inflation, but that's the only one of the social evils you can avoid. Because of the increase in population, there are many areas in which there simply isn't room for everyone. Schools have to double shift, and your chances for getting a child into a day-care center are about as good as taking a sunbath in January. Coupled with the present social pressure to work and have money, this shortage of daycare has lead to widespread child neglect. Both mothers and fathers have to work, or feel that they have to, and so hundreds of children are left to fend for themselves.

At the same time, the new Dodge Wagon that so many people can finally afford doesn't look so shiny as it once did. The traffic is so bad that you might as well be walking, just like back in the old days. While the population has quadrupled, and the car population has more than quadrupled, the number of streets has remained virtually the same. I used to do a lot of hitchhiking in the pre-pipeline days, and because there wasn't much traffic I often walked all the way into town from my place four miles out. It took me about an hour. Since the pipeline came to town, my funky old road has become a major highway, and it sometimes takes me longer than an hour to *drive* to town. I'm not sure I've gained anything by being able to afford a vehicle, and I may well have lost.

When it comes to pollution, Fairbanks is in a class by itself. Anchorage and other cities have become polluted too, but it is Fairbanks, because of the ice fog, which is really a serious case.

It used to be that in a place where there were some signs of advanced civilization—cars, a power plant, etc.—the ice fog would set in at about forty below zero and get worse as the temperature dropped lower. Ice fog occurs when it gets so cold that the water vapor in the air crystallizes and produces a shimmering mass very much like fog. The more water vapor there is in the air (caused by increased population, buildings, and vehicles), the worse the ice fog will be. And ice fog is misery.

When ice fog occurs, it is bound to be very cold, and when it's very cold it's bound to be dark most of the time. And now on top of the cold and the dark, you can't see across the street even during the few precious daylight hours. During the ice fog you have to know downtown Fairbanks well, or you'll get lost. And traffic accidents are a dime a dozen. As well, added to the condition of zero visibility, this iced-in atmosphere holds all common pollutants close to the ground. Carbon monoxide and sulfur dioxide counts that are in the danger area are simply to be lived with.

Ice fog used to set in at about forty below and get worse as the temperature decreased, but as the amount of water vapor in the air increases, the critical temperature approaches closer to zero. Now, at zero or ten below, you can see the beginnings of ice fog in Fairbanks. And as each year it sets in at a higher temperature, so also does it spread over a larger area. When you have a house for sale in Fairbanks, it's in your favor to be able to include in the ad: "Out of the ice fog." Lately more and more people look like liars, as the ice fog spreads further and further. It now goes eight or ten miles up the road from Fairbanks toward Prudhoe Bay. And presumably will go further next year.

Besides the increased number of cars and houses, another cause of the ice fog is the Chena River, a little river that runs through the middle of Fairbanks. Like almost all rivers in the north, its natural state in the winter is frozen solid. But since there happens to be a power plant in the middle of town, and since this power plant cools down its turbines with water, and since this heated water is then dumped into the Chena River, the river doesn't freeze anymore. All winter a channel stays open, and a fog rises off it, spreads over the city, and freezes in the air. This power plant has dumped its warm water into the river for a long time, but in lesser amounts than recently. Due to the need to produce more power it had to be increased in size, and the result is ever-increasing ice fog.

The technology exists, or could exist shortly, to greatly reduce the ice fog problem. A study was done concerning the Chena River problem, and a solution arrived at: the hot water being dumped into the river could be used to heat a thousand homes in Fairbanks. A couple of inventors at the University of Alaska, working without funding, have found a way to reduce the water vapor in engine exhaust. Much of the problem could be solved by installing electrical outlets on the parking meters in the downtown area. That would allow people to plug in their engine circulating heaters during the coldest of the weather, when many people leave their cars idling so that they won't be frozen up when they return to them. At sixty below, it takes only two or three hours to make a car impossible to start.

But any of these solutions would cost money, and when it comes to that, no one has the money. Alyeska, it is true, has given the people of Alaska, some people at least, a lot of money. But it has also given them carbon monoxide counts that rival those of downtown Los Angeles during the smog days. It is my opinion that money should be forthcoming to remedy the problem. By holding out the offer of money, Alyeska has induced floods of people to come to almost all of Alaska's towns and cities. These people are needed: the pipeline can't be built without them. But meanwhile, the cities have been left in the lurch. The oil companies have done nothing substantial to remedy all the problems that they caused in the first place. Legally, of course, the oil companies are in no way responsible for the havoc they have created. That only suggests to me that there are some laws badly in need of change. Long ago it should have been made impossible to come into a city, turn it upside down, build your pipeline, and move on, ignoring social obligations throughout. If a foreign power had done what the oil companies have done, it would be termed an invasion. And yet, it has not only not been termed an invasion (many Alaskans call it precisely that), but the oil companies are being invited back to build another line, since they did such a good job on this one!

What has happened to Fairbanks, and to some extent to other cities as well, is that is has totally and radically changed. The entire character of the city is different from what it used to be. Fairbanks used to be considered by many as a good place to live. Now it is considered by all a poor place to live—but a great place to make money. The values of the residents have necessarily changed, the priorities have shifted. A few years back there was almost no one who would have admitted the truth of the axiom "Time is money." It simply didn't work that way. Time was available to everyone in abundance. There was always a day or two to help someone build his cabin or dig up his potatoes. There was always time to get in a little fishing or hiking or just talking.

Now, time is money. Everyone is busy. It takes a lot of money to live, and all the things that money can buy suddenly seem necessary, impossible to live without. If someone needs a week's help in putting a roof on a cabin, you have to put it in terms of money. You can help your friend for a week with his roof, or you can work on the pipeline and make a thousand dollars. A week, which used to be anything you wanted to make it, is now nothing more nor less than a thousand dollars.

It is impossible and pointless to try to tell what has changed. Everything has. Fairbanks used to be one of those places where you didn't have a lock on the front door. Now you're very likely to be robbed. Fairbanks *is* a great place to make money, and not only for business people. Thieves, card sharks, pimps, muggers and drug dealers are finding it a great place to make money, too. As soon as there's a single fool with money, half a dozen hustlers show up to try to take it away from him. Money rules.

I know that it is unfashionable to make lament for the good old days. Things change, and to say that the changes are better or worse is ultimately beside the point. The changes that have been brought to Alaska by the oil companies are nothing that hasn't happened before. America has come to Alaska, as it has come to so many little areas on the fringes of America. A few years ago there was something of the pioneering spirit left in Alaska, and now not much more than the myth remains. While the island was there, it was a pleasant island, and served the needs of those people who liked to live a little ways out from America. But when America hit, it hit hard, and it was so obvious what was happening because the change took only a couple of years. What might have come to pass little by little over the next fifty years happened in the ugliest possible fashion in only a few years. The result was colliding cultures, pipeline impact, instantly Americanized Alaska. Now there are no more islands. I, among others, regret the loss.

How Pipeliners Spend Their Money

The wages that workers make while building the pipeline
have become legendary. Anybody who is willing and able
to work the whole year 'round can gross forty thousand
dollars, and a lot more than that if he gets the right job. By
working a standard seventy-hour week (known as seven
tens), you can pull down from a thousand to fifteen hundred
dollars. The wage scale now starts at $12.85 an hour for the
lowly laborer, and goes up to around $17.50 for a pipewel-
der, electrician, plumber, or ironworker. Everything over
forty hours is time and a half, Saturdays and Sundays are
time and a half even if you start work on Saturday morning,
and holidays pay double time. And in many cases, workers
put in more (or at least get paid for more) than seventy
hours a week. I clocked in with ninety-four hours one
week, and that is by no means a record. I've known
mechanics who've gotten over a hundred hours for several
weeks in a row.

One might wonder how this is possible, knowing that there are only 168 hours in a week. Well, besides the regular ten- or sometimes twelve-hour day, there is also travel time. It often takes two hours to get from the camp to the worksite when the road is rough and the driver is a "safety first" man, and though you don't get paid for all the hours spent on the bus, you do get paid for half of them. Ride to work on company time, come home on your own, is the rule. And then there's the matter of getting called out in the middle of the night. If you go home and eat dinner, watch a movie, and then have to go out and accomplish some super-high priority work, you get paid for four hours. Even if it only takes fifteen minutes. There's a fair amount of such work to be done, especially if the foreman likes nothing better than a happy crew. As the hours add up, so do the dollars.

The amount of money that can be made in one year by a worker in the right situation is truly phenomenal. I once knew an X-ray technician who was pulling down $2200 a week. Assuming that he worked forty weeks out of the year, that would add up to eighty-eight thousand dollars. Some other people who have it made are the long-haul Teamsters. It takes about twelve hours to make the run from Fairbanks to the Yukon River, but that run pays eighteen hours. And I know a man who has been making that run every day, seven days a week, for months. Likewise, there are many other drives where the Teamster can beat the time and make a lot of money without overworking.

I'd be the last to argue that pipeliners are overpaid. Besides the work itself, there are a lot of things to put up with, and working seventy or eighty hours a week is in no way to be compared to working a forty-hour week. No matter how soft the job, working ten hours every day for nine weeks is a grind. It takes a lot out of you. The work schedule calls for nine weeks of work, and then one week off, but that can be stretched to two if you apply ahead of time for an extended vacation, or R&R, as it is known. R&R is definitely needed after nine weeks on the job. There are some people who will go as long as eighteen weeks without any time off, but after eighteen weeks there's a mandatory vacation. I'm of the opinion that if you've made it eighteen weeks you're definitely pipeline crazy beyond repair. If you go that long you might as well stay, because you probably wouldn't be able to cope with anything else.

Be that as it may, it is indisputably true that pipeliners make a lot of money. As a matter of fact, they are the highest paid workers in the world. Whatever they may have to put up with to get that money, they do get it. And then comes the matter of spending it.

When speaking of the ways in which pipeliners spend their money, it is necessary to make the familiar distinction between Alaska pipeliners and those from the lower 48. The reason that the wages on the pipeline are so high is, of course, related to the high cost of living in Alaska, which has gotten much higher because of the pipeline. Wages have long been higher in Alaska than in other parts of the country, and even the minimum wage is higher than it is for the rest of the U.S. Alaskans need the high wages of the pipeline just to stay even. In addition, most of the young Alaskans who are working on the line were flat broke when they got their first jobs, living in that lifestyle known as "Alaska poor." Since I was one of them, I consider myself an expert on how this group spends its money.

To begin with, pipelining hippies don't work all year. Going to work is a necessary evil, but you only work when the evil is absolutely necessary. My case is probably average. I put in about four or five months out of the year, making twenty thousand dollars or so. The rest of the time is reserved for important things. But even for those who work longer than this the money is not hard to get rid of. First on the list of things to buy is a place to live. There are

hundreds and hundreds of Alaskans who during the first
year of the pipeline bought and paid for a piece of land, and
then built a house on it. It's the all-time favorite way to
spend your money. And next comes the four-wheel-drive
truck, which you need because you built your house so far
off the beaten path that there's no other way to get to it.

Since everything costs so much in Alaska, and since
Alaskans often aren't into working the whole year round,
we can usually spend our money on what we need or what
we think we need and that will take care of it. Part of the
lure of going to work on the pipeline is the notion (or pipe-
dream) that if you make enough money and play your cards
right, you may never have to work again—an infinitely ap-
pealing idea to many Alaskans, or anyone for that matter.
There are many, many people who are devoting their pipelining days to getting set, to buying the materials for a life-
support system that will then free them of the need for
money, and consequently the unpleasant necessity of working for such companies as ARCO and Exxon. These people
buy tons of tools, materials for greenhouses, wind-
generators, and lots of insulation for their houses. There is
always the hope that one day the pipeline will go away,
leaving hundreds of vacant buildings, which means lumber
for the scrounging. Who knows, you might even be able to
cash in on some unemployment insurance. The pipeline
must be one of the very few places where you can find
serious talk of retirement by people twenty-five to thirty
years old. Whether the plans will work or not I can't predict. When you've never had any money before, getting
hold of a large amount of it all at once can be dangerous.
There are a lot of detours on the road between the pipeline
and self-sufficiency.

For many of the older guys who are working steadily on
the line, this probably does represent the last employment
they'll ever have. If you have put in a sufficient number of

hours you can retire at age fifty-five from most unions, and collect a sizeable pension. And for the older guys, it may work. If you are willing to live cheaply—and many old time Alaskans don't know how to live any other way, having done it all their lives—savings of a hundred thousand dollars plus a seven or eight hundred dollar pension could very well take you to the end of your life. A good number of these old time construction men regard the pipeline and its high wages as a veritable godsend, and properly so. After not having been able to find much work for the last twenty or thirty years, their problems are solved. It works out very nicely for some.

When it comes to spending hard-earned money, the difference between the pro pipeliners and the Alaska contingent is very great. This is not to say that there are not a number of Southern pipeliners who have roughly the same goals and same reasons for working as the Alaskans. There assuredly are. There are some who are looking forward to retirement, some who are getting themselves set up on a farm that they hope never again to leave. But for the most part pipeliners are—well, pipeliners. That's what they do, build pipelines. And though I've never known one of them to turn down his paycheck, they are working as much because of the fact that there is a pipeline to build as they are for the money.

They tend to make a lot more money than the Alaskan workers. They have the highest paying jobs, and they stay on these jobs year 'round. Furthermore, the places they come from—Bald Knob, Arkansas, or Monroeville, Alabama—are some of the cheapest cities to live in you'll find in the United States. Most of the neighbors are getting by pretty nicely on ten thousand a year, and fifteen thousand puts you on the top of the heap. But there's old Ezra Jackson, working up there on the Alaska Pipeline, pulling down sixty thou a year, room and board included. What is a guy like this going to do with that kind of money?

Well, to begin with, it isn't quite sixty thousand that he actually has to spend. First of all, Uncle Sam gets his cut. The government (that's pronounced *guv'ment*), regularly snags about 40 percent of those wages, right off the top. Unlike many people who earn sixty thousand or more a year, the pipeliner has virtually no way of protecting his money. He has no one to entertain, and virtually no expenses. The IRS disallows the flights between Fairbanks and home every nine weeks, saying that he doesn't have to go home unless he wants to. At the same time, the cost of cold weather gear ($300-500) is disallowed; the IRS considering this the clothing that is required for a geographical location, not for a certain type of work. In short, there's very little to do to keep the "guv'ment" from ripping him off. The IRS has very little sympathy for a blue-collar worker who pulls down over fifty thousand a year.

But even after taxes there's a lot of money left; say thirty to forty thousand dollars, cold cash money. When the fellows back home are bringing in seven thousand dollars or so, thirty-five thousand is a hell of a lot. And the true pipeliner wants to spend that money. The true hard-drinking fist-throwing cowboy pipeliner ain't about to save any of that money, 'cause he knows if he does the "guv'ment" is gonna get it, one way or the other. If there's one thing the hard core pipeliner knows about economics, it's that the money you earn this year won't be worth a damn next year. Money's meant to be spent.

However, that is a hell of a lot of money just to spend. Especially if your idea of high style is a double-wide mobile home and a Sunday suit from the Sears catalogue. The problem is that people who make sixty thousand a year usually have developed some rather expensive tastes along the way. Not so with the pipeliner. He has been schooled from birth in the fine art of gracious poverty. If push comes to shove, he knows how to live on next to nothing, and he doesn't really have any desires that it takes massive infuions of money to fulfill. Pipeliners think of themselves as poor, they expect to remain poor, and they take steps to guarantee this expectation will become reality.

During one of those interminable bullshit sessions in some warm-up shack or another, I remarked to a welder, "Bill, if I had your kind of money I sure as hell wouldn't be working."

"Money!" exclaimed Bill. "I ain't got no money. If I did I'd be heading home to mama right away, but there's one thing I've always said—'I hate to fuck a hungry woman.' "

That is a line that I heard more than once. However, the fact remains that pipeliners *do* make a lot of money. And it is also true that they tend to consider themselves poor.

Pipeliners buy cars. They do not, however, buy Cadillacs, which are known to be hard to park, or Mercedes, which are made by scab foreigners. They stick with Fords and Pontiacs, and they usually seem to have a brother or a cousin who'll sell them one cheap. Thirft is a way of life when the depression is just behind the last hill. Strangely enough, this philosophy seems to be contagious. I was hitchhiking back to my house from the airport, just off the plane from Old Man Camp, $5,000 hot dollars in my pocket. The idea of taking a cab never occurred to me. Cabs are too expensive. I don't use them no matter how much money I have.

The pipeliner is rather limited in the ways that he can spend his money. He'll buy a camera, but he has no use for one of those fancy Japanese jobs that you have to be an engineer to operate. So he buys a Polaroid SR-70. That's sixty bucks well spent. In the same way, he'll go out to dinner, but there's something about fried chicken and mashed potatoes that makes Colonel Sanders seem like the ideal eating place. And so long as there's Budweiser he ain't about to shell out no fifty dollars for a bottle of wine. I once watched a crane operator in a Fairbanks restaurant attempt to teach a couple of his buddies how to eat escargots. He gingerly picked up the utensils and drawled to his friends, "Now boys, you watch careful, cause I'm gonna teach you how to rig a snail."

"That's quite a lash-up, all right," drawled an impressed buddy in reply.

And there are other things that the pipeliner couldn't quite bring himself to buy. He could easily afford a seventy thousand dollar house, but he would feel funny living in one. Besides, the neighbors would probably be some snooty doctors or lawyers or even psychiatrists, for chrissakes! He'll stick with his fifteen thousand dollar mansion at the end of Robert E. Lee Avenue.

The abstract idea of travel appeals to some pipeliners. But when he comes right down to it, there isn't really anywhere to go. If a man's been working on pipelines for a while he's most likely been to Louisiana, Texas and Oklahoma. Probably Michigan, Kansas, and Arizona. Maybe even Pennsylvania and Washington. He doesn't want to go to New York or San Francisco, having heard rumors about the class of people that live there. Foreign travel is another matter entirely. It is well-known that the French are snooty; there are Krauts in Germany, and he was there during the war anyhow. The British drink their beer warm, and the Commies are taking over Italy. He's already been to Iran and had his fill of A-rabs. Now Japanese hookers, that's something. But nobody talks English there, right? And so for travel the pipeliner will probably pack the family into the camper and head out to Disneyland. Or maybe just go fishing.

Since the things that he buys are cheap, he buys lots of them. Dozens of $6.98 shirts from Penny's. Rifles and fishing gear from the Sears catalogue. A couple or three fifty-dollar watches. Eight-track tape decks, and surely a C.B. radio lash-up. And a freezer to put meat in, just in case he ever gets time to go hunting. And gadgetry. Mechanics' tools that are never meant to be used, power saws that will never cut a board. But still, even with all that buying, that $700 or $800 a week take-home pay does add up.

If you don't believe in saving it and don't know how to spend it, you've got to throw it away. I knew a fifty-year-old laborer who had it down to a science. He found that after working the standard nine weeks in a pipeline camp, he could move into a whorehouse outside of Anchorage for a flat five hundred dollars a day, booze and breakfast *included*. He recommended this place highly. "You ain't never seen a covey like this one," he spouted. "They take care of you. Breakfast in bed, your pick of the girls, and all the fucking booze you can put down. I'd fuck one of those whores while I ate another, and don't ever let anybody tell you that there's anything wrong with eating a little fresh pussy." He'd just spent a week in the whorehouse. Now he was enlisting his fellow workers to go there with him next time R&R came around. It had proven a damned good way of getting rid of money.

Besides the flat fee of $3500, the brothel had an attached gambling room where he could get rid of anything left over. He'd gone there with forty-five hundred dollars, and come back to camp owing the house an extra two thousand. Now he was back at work, paying off the two thousand, and this time making plans for staying *two* weeks in the house. "Those girls loved me," he said. "They wanted me to stay longer."

Sex is one thing you can always spend money on, if you're of a certain inclination, and most pipeliners are. They are of almost universal agreement that sex costs money. The wife is a long ways away eight or nine months out of the year, and it takes a lot of money to keep her going. To a certain mentality, this is a clear case of paying for sex. And the hell of it is, you don't know whose sex you're paying for. There's a standard consolation for the welder who's fretting about the little woman back in Tallulah: "Don't you worry, Jack, I bet you'll find that cunt just the way you left it—freshly fucked."

The price of a Fairbanks quickie fluctuates, but it never seems to go below fifty dollars. Pipeliners resent having to put out that kind of money for sex, but they are resigned to it. "There's no fucking way," says a crane operator, "that I'd put out a hundred dollars for a piece of ass—unless I was horny or something." But what the hell, you're always paying for sex, whether in the form of a house on a hill or with hundred dollar bills, and what's a hundred dollar bill when you make one every day. Judging from the burgeoning Fairbanks hooker population, there's a lot of pipeline money that goes into paying for sex.

Sex, however, is not the only thing that a pipeliner can throw away his money on, or even necessarily the most popular. There is always gambling. Now gambling is not exactly legal in Alaska, nor is it exactly legal in the pipeline camps. But on the other hand, gambling is a way of life in the pipelining business, and "ain't nobody never stopped old Pete McCoy from a friendly game of cards, nor gonna."

The poker tables are set up in the recreation halls, and everybody agrees that's the best place for them. Experience shows that when you set to playing in a man's room, somebody's likely to get hurt before the night's over, and that doesn't do anybody any good. These boys take their poker seriously, and considering the sums involved, it's understandable.

The favorite game is usually something like seven card stud, because that'll get a lot of money out on the table. Stick to a twenty-dollar card limit so nobody will get out of line. Bluffing will get you nowhere, because everybody's in. You can raise three times, and three times it is, on every card. Sometimes they'll play progressive, trips to win, and then you can really get some money out. But what the hell, everybody's got the money, or at least knows someone he can borrow it from. Almost any night of the week you can see paychecks being grudgingly signed over and eagerly pocketed. I don't know this for a fact, but they tell me that there are some guys who make more at the poker table than they do at their jobs. And of course that sort has to get rid of it *real* fast, before the IRS finds out.

But along with the big winners go the big losers. There seem to be a couple of guys hanging out in every camp who have been there since the camp opened, are currently broke, and will probably leave the camp broke when the job folds. These are the sort who start drinking immediately after work, if they didn't start right after lunch, and come to the poker table barely able to see the cards. I'm not sure what they get out of losing every week's paycheck at the poker table, but at least it gives them a reason for working and keeps them out of trouble.

Most of the players, however, manage to break even. They win a couple hundred one night, drop it the next, and so it goes. I have seen it happen on a few occasions that on the night before leaving for R&R, the couple hundred that was lost turned out to be intended plane ticket money, and it was necessary to spend another week in camp. The big thrill about money won at poker is that nobody knows about it, including the wife, so if you win big before going home, you'll be sure to have some extra cash—and then you can get into some more poker games. Amaze the guys next door by betting the limit on every hand. And if you lose it, you can afford to be a graceful loser.

Another form of gambling, somewhat more respectable but ultimately amounting to the same thing, is known as investing. And pipeliners are investors. So far as the art is understood, investing is something you do when you have more money than you can spend. It's also a way of getting something for nothing. Pipeliners are heavy into investments.

On the pipeline there are as many con artists as there are potential investors. Get rich quick schemes abound. "Florida swamp? Where do I sign? Can't lose in real estate." Besides the real estate, another big favorite is mining, always a tricky business at best. Someone who looks more or less like a miner shows up in camp, shows off a few gold nuggets from his "mine," and he's in business. It definitely sounds like a way to get rich quick, and there's a certain romance to being part owner in an Alaska gold mine, although it often turns out that the "miner" does more of his work in Las Vegas than at his sluice box.

Pipeliners tend to invest in real things. Wien Consolidated, the airline that carries the workers back and forth from Fairbanks to the camps, is heavily favored with their investments. They're obviously doing a land office business, and guys are always quitting and getting new jobs, so it must be a good investment. Commodities futures, on the other hand, are something to stay strictly away from. A handful of paper don't mean shit—all pipeliners know about Confederate money.

This is not to say that there are not some who invest shrewdly and profitably. There are certainly many who are working to buy the farm next to theirs, who are getting set up in business, or doing any one of a hundred things that are considered reasonable and wise. But then again there are the others.

I was eating breakfast one morning when a pipeliner joined me, eating and reading the paper at the same time. "How's the stock market doing?" I asked him.

"I don't know shit about stocks," he declared. "I put my money strictly into houses and lots."

"Oh, so you like real estate?"

"Well, what I mean to say by that, son," he drawled, "is that I invest in whorehouses and lots of whiskey."

I certainly have no statistics, but I'd venture a guess that more pipeliner money goes into "houses and lots" investments than any other kind.

The whole problem of pipeliners and their money is an uncommon one—the case of a man with beer tastes and a champagne pocketbook. The nouveaux riches can find endless baubles to spend their money on, but they are fortunate in having wealth which is seemingly without end. The pipeliner is assuredly better off if he doesn't get used to living rich, because one day the pipeline is going to dry up and the next job may be hard to find. Layoffs and rumors of layoffs provide a constant reminder of that possibility, and so the pipeliner never gets into the habit of thinking of himself as rich; he simply spends it while he's got it.

I knew a husband and wife team who were almost overcome by having so much more ready cash than they'd ever had before. Dick was a pipefitter, and Betty was a waitress, which can be a very high paying occupation in Alaska. Between the two of them, they were grossing nearly a hundred thousand a year. And what did they do with that money? They bought. They had an apartment with the spare bedroom completely full of boxes of toys for a two-year-old grandchild. They had a garage full of hunting, fishing, and camping gear, tools, gadgets, a shallow water gold dredge, and a motorcycle. Betty had gone crazy with a Wards catalogue; Dick bought out the Penney's store. Chests of drawers were stuffed with new shirts and slacks that Betty had bought for Dick, and which he had no intention of wearing. Their entire savings consisted of the change that Betty had gotten in tips and put into a suitcase. When I last saw them they were trying to get out of Fairbanks before winter set in, but they were going to have to go back to work for a while in order to pay the freight charges to get all their stuff back home. "What happened to all your money?" I asked Dick.

"Oh, it just kind of disappeared."

As one who worked on the pipeline for a good while and came away *owing* a large amount of money, I can affirm that it does just disappear. Money doesn't seem to be worth much when you can make it at a rate of a thousand a week and get rid of it just as quickly. You take to eating all your meals in restaurants and leaving twenty-dollar tips, going to Hawaii for extended vacations, or anything else you might feel like doing. Easy come, easy go. Making money on the pipeline has been for many people, if nothing else, an interesting experience. Some have set themselves up for life, some have had a good time, and almost all have been, for thirty minutes at least, the richest man in the bar.

Dragging Up

The construction industry in general has a much higher employee turnover rate than, say, a bank, an automobile factory, or even a hamburger stand. Jobs are always starting and stopping, workers quitting and taking new jobs. It's a very fluid situation, as they say. But in the building of the Alaska pipeline, the turnover rate is even higher than in the rest of the construction industry. There are two main reasons for this. The first is that you earn enough money so that it usually isn't necessary to work the whole year around, even when there's work available, which is unusual in construction. And the second reason is that it's so easy to get another job. During the past couple of years, there's never been any problem with that. Once you're firmly entrenched in your union, you can almost certainly get another job if you choose to quit, and often with the same contractor that you quit on.

For both these reasons, pipeline workers are to a man ready to quit their jobs if that seems like the thing to do at

156

the moment. And when that is the case, the employer loses a lot of his traditional power over the employee. If there were no employee in the United States that was in fear of getting fired, the working situation would be a whole lot different from what it is. Just imagine what it would be like not to have a care whether you had a job or not tomorrow. Your boss comes along and tells you to type up these letters or sweep that floor or sell them cars or get started on that new ad campaign for the non-sticky roll-on deodorant. And if you should happen not to feel like doing the particular task, you would feel perfectly free to say, "Why don't you take your letters, your broom, your car, and about half a case of this sticky roll-on deodorant and shove it all up your ass." If he fires you, that's fine. More power to him. Let him find some other idiot to do silly jobs.

That's pretty much the situation on the Alaska pipeline. A small management revolt last year produced a poster which was circulated throughout the camps: "Management respectfully requests that all employees take a shower before reporting for work. Since we have to kiss your asses, we'd like them to be clean." Now that's the sort of management/worker compromise I can get behind.

Since the majority don't much care whether they're working on their present job or some other or none at all, workers drag up a lot. Now, you won't find the verb "to drag up" in your dictionary, but a reasonable definition might be "to quit a job, especially without notice." I'm not sure that anyone knows the etymology of the word, but I'd guess that it was formerly sea lingo, having to do with dragging up anchor. At any rate, on the pipeline it means that you're quitting, as does "to pull the pin," which is almost as common. But dragging up is more than simply quitting a job—it's the *art* of quitting a job. And the skills of this art have been honed to a fine edge on the pipeline.

There are three basic ways to be *terminated*, as the bureaucratese goes. When you leave a job, you receive a termination slip, or pink slip, and the circumstances of the termination are spelled out thereon. First of all you can be fired. This manner of leaving a job isn't all that common on the pipeline, and I never could manage to get myself fired, though I gave it a try a couple of times. The bosses are willing to put up with a lot. Most foremen won't fire you for telling them to fuck themselves, and being fired for not doing your job is not all that common either, except in the case of women, to whom it happens all the time. An incorrigible rowdy might get fired, especially if the foreman bears the brunt of his rowdyism. I met a tall Indian who claimed to have been fired from ten different jobs, each time for punching out the bossman. But still, getting fired isn't all that common. That's partly because workers quit so fast they don't give themselves a chance to be fired.

Now the superior method of leaving a job is the lay-off. Everyone's gunning for a lay-off. It carries with it many advantages. First of all, if you're so inclined, you can begin to collect unemployment insurance immediately. And if you should want to go back to work for the same company, they will probably facilitate you when work comes up. If you get laid off after having worked on a job for less than seven days, you can return to your old place on the union list, instead of going to the bottom of the list, which is the case when you quit or get fired. So getting laid off has its advantages, but it isn't easy to do. It can take some finagling to have your termination slip marked "Lay off—reduction in force—eligible for rehire." Unless there is an actual reduction in force, which doesn't happen nearly often enough, you have to be in good with the bossman to get yourself laid off.

But of all the ways of terminating a job, dragging up is the most glorious. When you decide on Wednesday that you're going to drag up on Sunday evening, right when the work week ends, you are definitely in control. You don't care if you get fired, you don't care if the world passes you by, because you've decided you're going to drag up and nobody can stop you. When you drag up you can receive one of two judgments: Eligible for rehire, or ineligible for rehire. The simple act of quitting without notice is in most cases not enough to give you an ineligible for rehire rating. I quit on H.C. Price three times after having worked less than a week, and each time I was proclaimed eligible for rehire. "The boy don't work for long, but he gives her hell while he's around."

When you drag up you have to supply your employer with a reason for quitting. A great deal of creative effort goes into coming up with a truly unique reason for quitting. One of the finest, which has practically become legend, was that of a laborer at Pump Station Number Eight, twenty-odd miles southeast of Fairbanks. This laborer came to work, noticed that the sun was shining and the birds were singing, and said to himself, "It's a beautiful day. What am I doing working on the pipeline?"

He considered this for a moment, found his foreman, and said, "Jack, I'm dragging up."

"Well, how come you're doing that?" asked Jack. "You're one of my best workers."

"It's a beautiful day," replied the laborer.

And that was what went on the termination slip under the heading "Reason for quitting": "It's a beautiful day."

There are so few chances for creativity on the pipeline that manufacturing a unique and shocking reason for dragging up occupies idle minds for many an hour. You have to decide what effect you want to achieve. "Too many homosexuals on crew" will do one thing, and "Incipient inability to maintain erection" will do another. "Horny" has one effect, "Bored" another. The irony of "Too cold" is masterfully balanced by the earthy "Got the red ass." Having the red ass, by the way, refers in typical pipeliner fashion to being cranky, nasty, bitchy, or mean. The most conscious literary effort by a pipeliner thus far exists in a bit of doggerel left behind as a drag up message on an office chalkboard:

> My ass is red
> The grass is green
> There's lots of places
> I ain't seen.
> Adios, motherfuckers.

There is a story, and it may even be true, of a roughneck who quit a job back in the exploration and drilling days of the North Slope. It seems that a hole had been drilled down to a depth of eight thousand feet or so, and the roughneck one day happened to drop a wrench into the hole. When you get a wrench down at the bottom of a drill hole, progress comes to a standstill, the wrench has to come out. This is a long process, involving pulling the bit up, section by section, and then sending an instrument down to snag the wrench and pull it up. Then it's a matter of coupling the sections back together again and starting to drill once more. It took the crew a week to perform these tasks, and the whole of the week was sheer drudgery. The operation completed, the foreman moseyed up to this particular roughneck and said, "Pack your bag, son, we can't afford to have hands like you on this job."

"Hey, you can't fire me," said the roughneck.

"Why not?" asked the foreman.

The roughneck ambled over to the hole, threw the same wrench in again, and replied to the foreman, "Because I quit!"

If the flair and flamboyance of this end-of-job scene has not been surpassed over the years of the pipeline fiasco, it is not because no one has tried to surpass it. After the insane and frustrating meaninglessness of a few weeks or months of working on the pipeline, you begin to get a monomaniacal urging that tells you that if nothing else has significance, at least the last day should. Crews spend day after day talking about how they'll quit. Perhaps the most moderate form of the drag up art is demonstrated in the mass-quitting ritual.

It is generally agreed upon by experts that the whole crew should quit at once, if that is convenient, if everyone is sufficiently pissed off and bored and sufficiently rich that it doesn't matter whether they work one more day or one more week. Jesus, I've been in the middle of some great drag up scenes. Sometimes the whole crew will go en masse to the foreman and a spokesman will say, "Jack, we ain't gonna put up with this bullshit no longer. We're going home." And Jack will shake his head and say, "Well, I guess if you gotta go, you gotta go."

Then there are the progressive drag ups, where the crew sits around and gets drunk and starts talking about California or Fairbanks or pussy and whiskey and decides to quit. The hands go one at a time to the foreman and tell him sort of confidential-like that for purely personal reasons they have to leave on Monday morning and he's been a great old boy to work with but you know how things are, and can you get me a plane ticket and put down "reduction in force" on the termination slip. After about the fourth or fifth one the bossman, if he's got anything left in his head at all, begins to get suspicious, and at lunchtime will mention that if anyone wants to go home on Monday he'd better say something pretty quick because there might not be any room on the plane. Everyone grins, and every half hour the poor bossman has to write out another termination slip.

The hope which a whole crew has in quitting at once is that the pipeline will be shut down. Just why this seems like such a good idea is not immediately clear to me from the perspective of my study, but after a month or two of work it does definitely seem like a good idea. The mechanics get to feeling powerful and important and realize, "This crew can't run even a single day without us." And so they all quit and hang around the union hall, waiting for the call, "Green Construction needs three mechanics, and be ready to get on the plane *to*night!" And then one of the mechanics who quit can nudge the guy next to him and say, "I was one of the mechanics who quit. We flat shut 'em down. That's why they need somebody in a hurry."

Perhaps it will seem to some that trying to shut a job down by quitting without notice is not a moderate action. And I would agree, except that when compared to other favored methods of dragging up, the former does take on the pale gleam of moderation.

The aim is to get even and to be remembered. Now a laborer is not likely to be remembered as a hell of a hole digger. But if, in addition to being a hole digger par excellence, he should break the handles of an even hundred shovels on his last day of work, this would be somewhat memorable, or at least remembered. But laborers have little power. They control no huge machines, and the destiny of critical operations does not often lie in their hands. Laborers are for the most part confined to dragging up in large numbers. The mastery of this part of the fine art of dragging up resides largely with the laborers.

Now when it comes to doing some impressive damage, one must turn to the equipment operators. These men daily drive around on machines that cost up to a quarter of a million dollars, and some of the orn'rier ones have been known to drive that quarter million directly into a lake. Or into a wall. Down a mountain. Into a ditch. Through the warehouse. And after you've raised your blade and sent the D-8 on its way to the lake, the only appropriate thing to say is, "Fuck 'em if they can't take a joke."

That line is uttered constantly on the pipeline. It will cover any mistake, major or minor, intended or not. As the forklift driver said after he forgot to lower his forks and took out the back end of a warehouse (mid-winter, naturally), "Fuck 'em if they can't take a joke."

As the surveyor who kicked down the project superintendent's office door after having hard words with the foreman said, "Fuck 'em if they can't take a joke."

One night in Prudhoe Bay a couple of mechanics got a wild hair up their ass and decided to drive to Fairbanks. Since they had a pickup idling outside and a hundred-gallon gas tank, they figured it would be easy enough to stumble outside and drive off. They got about a quarter of a mile before the truck of its own accord went into the ditch. They figured that unless they got that pickup back to camp they'd be in a shitload of trouble, so they wandered back to camp and got into a diesel-powered four-wheel-drive five-ton rig and put it into the ditch only a few yards from the pickup. Now they figured they would *really* be in a shitload of trouble. But fortunately there happened to be a 998 front-end loader idling in the yard and its exhaust looked like the halo of salvation. They drunkenly clambered into it, ran into a pickup, took a shortcut across the tundra, buried it in five feet of snow, hiked back to camp and continued drinking.

"Tough luck, Ben," I said to one of them as they sat at breakfast the next morning in the custody of two security guards who were ushering them to the airport.

"Fuck 'em if they can't take a joke," growled Ben.

If the laborers have the edge when it comes to quitting en masse, and the operators have it in the area of destroying huge machines, the pipewelders are masters of subtlety. The pipewelders are likely to get into some playful mischief at any time. They glory in little touches like welding someone's lunch bucket to a sideboom. But when it comes to dragging up, they can be downright dangerous. There are rumors that at various times, various objects have been welded inside pipelines. Nothing big, you understand.

Nothing like a forty-eight-inch-diameter circle of steel. Just little things like a chipping hammer or an odd chunk of iron that was lying around. Not very big, surely not big enough to stop the flow of the oil, but big enough to stop the "pig" that is sent through the line to root out anything which may be inside it. Big enough to take a few days of work to remove.

As a foreman once told me, "There's one thing I know about pipeliners. If you're trying to build a pipeline, you'd do best not to piss them off."

The possibility of dragging up is what makes working on the pipeline different from going to prison. Even given the big paychecks, given the fun and the fucking around, the dope, the booze, the gambling, given the pool tables and the nightly movie it is still damned difficult to stay in a pipeline camp. Just like prisoners, the inmates mark their calendars. Practically any man on the job can tell you to the day how long he's been in camp, when his next R&R is due, and his opinion on whether he'll make it that long or not. No matter how many luxuries a pipeline camp might boast, there's no way it's going to fool anyone into thinking it's home. It's a place where you put in your time and leave as quickly as possible.

Part of the ritual of getting through the day is to talk about going home. All day long we remind each other that this isn't going to last forever—in ten days or forty-five, it's time to go home. It can get to the point where each morning you have to make a decision about whether you're going to work or not. Once that happens, you're bound to drag up pretty soon. If you go to camp with a firm resolve to stay nine weeks, and a pressing debt as encouragement, then you might make it. But if you go to camp planning to stay till you can't take it anymore, then you'll probably be home inside a month.

You can always count on encouragement from your fellow workers to leave. LeRoy the Welder says, "Well, I called up my old lady last night, and I told her, 'Sarah Jean, I'm coming home, and when I get there I don't want you to have nothin' on but the radio, and that better be turned down low.' "

And then I can't resist. "Damn, I wish I was home in Fairbanks instead of hanging out in this godforsaken place."

"Well, why don't we go down on the same airplane," suggests LeRoy. "I bet this crew could get along without you."

"I imagine they could," I admit.

"And then we could go down to the Bare Affair and look them ladies over and get right fucked up."

"Well, I think I'll stay till the weekend at least."

But in reality there have been half a dozen such times that I didn't make it till the weekend. It always happened that I reached a point where it didn't seem to matter whether I stayed on the job or went home, and at that point I always drug up. The more jobs I worked at, the quicker that point came. From working on the Alaska pipeline, I came to see the whole idea of working in a different light.

Those who write about working in this country hold two diametrically opposed opinions about the situation. One group claims that the workers are in reality unhappy with their lot, and that many changes need to be made. The other group says that although workers bitch a lot, they really like their work and in fact wouldn't know what to do without it. The phenomenon of the Alaska pipeline should provide a few relevant observations.

The workers on the Alaska pipeline, who are higher paid than any others, also quit their jobs more often that any other workers. There are very few men who work twelve months out of the year, and they are regarded by their fellow workers with a variety of feelings: awe, dismay, the assumption that they must be out of their gourds, or the realization that they must be in desperate need of money. I feel certain that most people don't work the year round for the simple reason that the high pay makes that unnecessary. If workers generally could make enough money in six months that they could live on it all year, the majority would work half the year. On the pipeline it is apparent that there are some—mostly older men who are unable to think of themselves as anything but workers—for whom the job has meaning. These guys are likely to work most of the year, but they will often take extended vacations. The young people who work on the pipeline see the job as nothing more than a way of getting money, and probably a slightly unethical way at that. And they work only so long as it takes to get the money they need. The work itself is thought of as absurd, a waste of time, and part of a project that never should have been started in the first place.

Workers keep working because they have to—they can't live without the money. Any tom-foolery about workers liking to work could easily be disproven by giving workers higher wages and then watching them quit. The idea that there is something fulfilling about working for an oil company or General Motors is nothing other than propaganda designed to convince workers to keep working. As so many pipeline workers have found out, unemployment is a very natural and comfortable state for humans—when you don't have to worry about how to pay the rent. The idea that people don't know what to do when they have leisure time is also propaganda. It's very true that people who work eight or ten hours a day don't do anything creative after work or on weekends. But that is because they live in the shadow of their jobs.

Working makes you stupid and unaware. You have to become something of a slave to work as a manual laborer, unless, of course, you are working for yourself. It doesn't surprise me at all that people who retire or try out a twenty-hour work week have problems filling up empty time. Working teaches you to be an idiot, teaches you never to act unless the bossman tells you to. After a while you give up asking whether it's expedient or intelligent or useful to do what you are told—you simply do it. Work forms in you the mentality of a laboratory monkey: pull the lever, out comes a paycheck. After having done that all your life it is not surprising that you know how to do nothing else.

Almost any morning on the pipeline there can be heard the cynical voice of a worker pretending he is the foreman: "All right boys, let's get out there and save America. Them folks down there in the lower 48 are gonna flat freeze their asses next winter if we don't get them some oil."Practically all the workers, including the conservative ones, believe that they are working on a job which has no other purpose than to make a lot of money for the oil companies and their friends. It's difficult to get very excited over such a lofty purpose as this. I think that workers could get excited about their work if it were in fact honest work, if it were useful. But no matter how much P.R. hype Alyeska puts out about the pressing need for Alaska's oil, few workers are convinced that they are doing anything that really needs doing. It's just a way to make money. To make money you have to sell your time, and you might as well sell it to the highest bidder. And when you've sold as much as you can spare, you drag up.

On the last job I had on the pipeline I worked with a VSM crew, pounding forty-foot lengths of pipe into the ground with a Becker hammer drill. I knew that it was my last job—I had already decided that it would be more fun, if less profitable, to write about the pipeline than to work on it. But since it was my last job, I found myself completely unable to put up with any of the normal pipeline bullshit. I was ready to get into a shouting match with the foreman anytime he was. I had never before been fired from a pipeline job, and instead of looking upon that possibility as a grave evil, I actually felt that it would help to round out my work record. Somebody who's never been fired is likely to be thought of as a company man. God forbid!

One night I got into it with the foreman, an old-time Texas equipment operator named Dick. I was trying (but not very hard) to explain that a piece of work we were engaged in was completely useless, and that if he'd ever worked in cold weather before he'd realize that. At one point he looked at me and asked in his most philosophical drawl, "Son, have you ever held down a job before?"

I drawled back at him, "Dad, I've been taking care of myself since I was sixteen, and I have held down any number of jobs. As a matter of fact I've never been fired from one, but I would be especially proud to be fired by you."

"Shucks," he said, "I don't want to fire you, I just want you to do your job."

I wandered off, thought about it for a while, looked up Dick again and told him I'd decided I was going to drag up.

"I can't blame you," he said. "I've been considering the same thing myself." He convinced me to stay one more day so he could get a laborer to replace me. But the next morning when I got on the bus, one pipeliner immediately offered to fight me on general principles, and the Cat skinner vowed that if he caught me out on the right-of-way mopping up the numerous small oil spills, he'd run me over with his Cat. "I don't have to put up with this bullshit," I told the laborer sitting next to me. "I've got money in the bank." When the bus made its nightly stop at a handy liquor store, I decided that I was done pipelining. "Tell old Dick I won't be in tonight," I said to my laborer buddy. "Tell him the whole thing's a joke, and fuck him if he can't take a joke." I stepped out the back door of the bus and set off walking for home.

A few days later I wandered into the office to pick up my paycheck. No one there seemed to know that I'd quit.

They advised me to go find my foreman. "Oh shit," I thought. "Typical bureaucracy."

As I started down the long hall I ran into Dick. "Hey, boss," I said, "how about filling out a termination slip for me?"

"I'm afraid I can't do that," he said. "I drug up myself yesterday."

"Well, congratulations! What are you going to do now?"

"Oh, I think I'll go back home and look over my cattle. You?"

"I've been working on a book about the pipeline for a while," I said. "I think I may have time to put it together now."

"Well, that sounds real fine," he drawled. "Be sure and put me in it. And, Ed, remember . . . Fuck 'em if they can't take a joke."

Afterword

When I finished the manuscript of this book and handed it to the publisher, thoughts of the midnight sun began to prey heavy on my mind. When it comes to sheer rowdyism and energetic debauchery, there is no place to match Fairbanks in the summertime. There is something in Fairbanks that lends itself to binges that last far into the next day. Perhaps it is the prevailing spirit of anarchy, perhaps it is the sun cracking the horizon at one o'clock in the morning, perhaps it is the fact that the bars are open until five o'clock in the morning that makes time seem meaningless and one more joint seem like the best of all possible ideas. Aside from two weeks of completely unhinged irresponsibility and partying with people that I hadn't seen for six months, I also had some serious business to conduct.

I had subscribed to a Fairbanks newspaper while vacationing and writing in California, but I felt out of touch with the real inside scoop that you get when you talk to pipelin-

170

ers daily and listen to the gossip. And there was one fact I felt was missing: the number of people killed on the job while building the pipeline.

Four tequila sunrises happier than I was when I left Oakland, I met a real live pipeliner shortly after boarding the plane in Seattle. He was a truck driver, as I remember, a Missouri boy. I asked him if you had to work when you signed up on a pipeline crew these days.

"Why sure you do," he said. "They don't give all that money away for nothing."

I mentioned that I myself had earned a large amount of pipeline money while producing next to nothing.

His face broke out in a grin. "Well, who'd you work for, good buddy?" he asked. "Me, I'm a Price man. Worked for 'em two years now. Well, I'll tell you how things are. They're trying to crack down. A couple weeks back they done fired eighteen guys for sleeping on the bus. The fact is, you still don't have to work, but you've got to be real cagey about looking like you're working. You know? Shuffle around a little, look like you're doing something important. Things haven't changed much." I heard from five different sources that eighteen guys had been fired for sleeping on a bus, but no one seemed to know of any other similar cases. Things hadn't changed much.

The Fairbanks Airport was as crowded as usual. The only car I could rent was a filthy '75 Gremlin that shook and rattled and pulled to the right every time I hit the breaks. Sixteen dollars a day, sixteen cents a mile, and a two hundred dollar deposit. I headed down Airport Road and immediately got lost. Lots of roadwork going on in Fairbanks these days. Most of the major streets in and around town are torn up, in the process of being turned into four-lane freeways, and in the meantime the citizenry drives uncomplainingly on totally unmaintained, jerrybuilt gravel by-passes. Shit, it's just like back in the fifties. Wasn't nothin' paved then, either.

"Ed McGrath, welcome back!" shrieked my friend Elaine as I walked down the path to her two-story, 12×16 shack, carrying my Kelty pack.

Elaine lives with Michael, who gave me sound advice about writing this book. I was anxious to find out what he'd have to say about it.

We got down to some serious dope smoking and talking. Michael and Elaine were absolutely amazed at my stories of life in California, blown away by the mention of twelve-mile long traffic jams, insane killers and junkies, huge brush fires and water shortages. "California's burning, awright!" said Michael. We watched the sun set, checked out the twilight, rejoiced in the dawn, and smoked another joint as the sun rose. It was one-thirty A.M. Elaine sifted through a huge stack of newspaper articles about the pipeline that she had been saving for me. "There's one thing I haven't been able to find out," she told me. "The number of people killed on the pipeline. I've talked to everybody who ought to know, and nobody's talking."

"How about Larry Carpenter?" Carpenter is one of Alyeska's PR men, and is currently making his debut in state politics.

She whipped out a notebook. "I talked to him on the phone and wrote it all down in case you'd want to see it."

I read the notes:

Elaine: Mr. Carpenter, would you tell me how many people have been killed on the pipeline?

Carpenter: Why do you want to know?

Elaine: I'm writing a book.

Carpenter: We don't give out that information.

Elaine: Why not?

Carpenter: We just don't.

Elaine: Could you tell me anybody who'd know?

Carpenter: Nobody knows.

Elaine: I'd just like to ask you: do you know yourself?

Carpenter: I'm not going to tell you that.

"It's a well kept secret," said Elaine. "I talked with Richard Fineberg about it, and he can't find out. I've tried a lot of different people, and either they don't know or they're not talking."

"I'll find out," I assured her at four o'clock in the morning. "I suspect it's a matter of buying drinks for secretaries."

The next morning I got up at nine, smoked a joint, and set off to find my Toyota pickup. When I left last December, I did everything in my power to take the doomed truck with me, but at fifty below zero there was no way that I could get it to run. It was getting about five miles to the gallon, the automatic choke having become convinced that it needed to do everything it could at that temperature. The hydraulic clutch was frozen stiff. I'd left it in my driveway and a character named Glen had promised to haul it out to his ten acres and retire it for the winter.

"How's my Toyota doing?" I asked him when I arrived.

"No problem," he said. "I worked on it for a couple of hours when the weather warmed up, and it runs just fine. I've been driving it around. Had to put a new condenser in it. I guess it's just a warm-weather truck."

"I guess," I said.

"Meanwhile," continued Glen, "I'm fixin' to put an addition on this house. You interested in working for a week?"

"Sure," I said. "I haven't done any honest work for six months now. It'd seem like a real vacation to get some blisters on my hands." We got right to work, raging around with his '53 Ford tractor, pulling down a woodshed which had been connected to the house. My job was to trot alongside the tractor with a piece of birch log and throw it in front of the tractor wheel if he was about to run into the house or knock down one of his kids. Seems he had ordered new brake linings for this ancient Ford a month or so ago, but they hadn't arrived yet. Ah, life on the frontier. Doing things the hard way.

We stopped work after a couple of hours to drink some beer. "I don't know," said Glen, "if I'm going to want to live here after I get this new addition built. Right up on the hill here they're planning to put in a trailer court. Probably be full of Texans. They're taking over the town, Ed. Even here, fifteen miles from the city limits, you're not safe. Have you seen all the new developments in Fairbanks? Goddamn, shopping centers and motels, refinery, new roads everywhere you look. I may just sell out after I get this building done. Probably get sixty, seventy thousand. I could buy a farm with that."

"It is absolutely insane," I agreed. "It's getting to look a lot like California around here."

After drinking a few more beers I set out to see some people who had been working on the pipeline. My buddy Paul is a good example of a Fairbanks hippie pipeliner. He's put in maybe six months of work out of the last two years, and goes to work mainly to sell the weed that he grows in his greenhouse. It turned out, as I visited around Fairbanks, that almost everybody is growing marijuana. It's practically legal, and no one seems to know of any busts. Fine crops of weed growing all around town. More weed than I had seen since I was a boy in Kansas and the public health officials came to our farm and told us they were going to defoliate our two acres of *cannabis Americana*. My dad was pleased about that. He was afraid it would do something terrible to the cattle. But that damned weed grew back the next year as strong as ever. Harder to stop than Russian thistle.

"Ah yes, the pipeline," mused Paul. "I worked for six weeks this spring and now I'm going to get electricity in my house. I feel like the pipeline is over with. It doesn't mean anything to me anymore. It's the same old shit. I worked a little when I was making my electricity money. Just a little. The whole thing is a mess, and I'm beginning to think that it won't be necessary for anyone to blow it up—it's going to tear itself apart. No matter what they say, an earthquake will probably do the job, and they don't have all the engineering worked out by any means. I've heard rumors too that the price is going up again."

"Oh really?" I said. "What's the new pricetag?"

"I don't know," said Paul. "I'd figure less than a billion more. They usually revise their estimates by less than a billion dollars."

Strangely enough, I read in the paper about two weeks later that the new official estimate is $7.7 billion, an increase of $700 million over the old figure. The original estimate, it will be remembered, was $800 million. Little things keep cropping up. The pricetag on the remedial pipe weld X-raying is estimated at $55 million. More pipe had to be ordered in order to skirt some problem terrain. And the pipe supports across the Yukon River bridge had to be redesigned and replaced. They tell me the boys down at the office clean forgot there was going to be oil in the pipe and designed the supports to hold the weight of the pipe alone. A forty-foot length of pipe weighs about 6,000 pounds. The oil inside it tips the scales at about 16,000. In another place when a short section of the pipeline was pressure tested with water, vertical support members sank up to seven inches. At the same time, concrete coated pipe has been floating to the top of rivers that it was installed in the bottom of. Presumably the weight of the oil will hold them down in the future. It all balances out, you see. Good enough for government work.

"What scares me," said Paul as we sat in his 1930-vintage cabin smoking homegrown, "is that this madness may never end. There's a natural gas pipeline that has to be built, and I've been hearing about a new oilfield east of

Prudhoe Bay. Then too, you can be sure that they'll declare a national defense emergency and open up the Navy's Pet 4 Reserve in the next few years. I imagine we'll see at least three new pipelines rampaging through here in the next ten years. I guess we'll have to learn to live with the Texans."

Alaskans may have to learn to live with the pipeline, but they don't have to like it. The crop of bumper stickers that I saw as I drove around Fairbanks gives testimony to their feelings. The oldest and most popular message reads: Alaska for Alaskans—Yankee go home.

Some specialize in a vicious humor: Happiness is ten thousand Okies going home—with a Texan under each arm.

Another advertises what may be an unfortunate truth: Alaskan resident—last of an endangered species.

And plastered everywhere are more bumper stickers: Let the bastards freeze in the dark, without Alaska oil.

And: Freezing in the dark builds character.

And then there are the Pipeline Jokes:

Q. How do you get fourteen Texans into a Volkswagen?
A. Just tell them it's going to Alaska.
Q. If a welder from Louisiana and a welder from Texas are driving opposite directions on the Alaska Highway at sixty miles an hour and they smash head on, who will die first?
A. Who gives a shit?
Q. Why do Texans fold the brims of their hats up?
A. So four of them can get into an Alyeska pickup.

Alyeska itself is the subject of occasional joking around. People far and wide refer to that corporate entity as "Uncle Al." Uncle Al, the rich one, you know. I asked a fellow where he'd gotten the expensive panelling he had in his living room. "From my uncle," he said. "Yup, old Uncle Al takes care of his boys."

Uncle Al, I found, had infuriated the locals by refusing to let them burn pipeline skids as firewood. There was a huge stack of them being burned just south of town. Somebody took a pickup load of them home with him and a few hours later had a state trooper knocking at his door. He had to reload the skids, take them back, and throw them into the bonfires. Alyeska certainly wouldn't want to take any business away from the local suppliers of firewood.

Aside from the fact that Alaskans don't like the invading outsiders, the relationship of the real Alaskan with unions is a very shaky one. As dyed-in-the-wool anarchists, one would think that Alaskans should have little use for the unions. And that to some extent is true. Working on a union job is bound to be a drag. All the work is departmentalized. As a laborer you dare not pick up a wrench to change a spark plug, even though the wrench is at hand and the mechanics are half a day away from the job. Union work doesn't fit very well into the Alaska tradition of knowing how to do almost everything; the tradition of busting out and doing whatever needs to be done. Union work involves all sorts of inanities.

Unions are conservative. They believe in jobs, no matter what the cost to the environment, no matter how utterly useless the jobs might be. They support political candidates who believe in jobs, even if at the same time these candidates are heavy into starting nuclear wars and keeping the minorities down. And unions deal in vast amounts of money and power, which generally indicates a certain amount of corruption, the proposition being that you can't come by that much money and power honestly.

On the other hand, union workers make lots of money. Alaskans, even real, honest, hard-assed, anarchist Alaskans, like to make lots of money, if it isn't too much trouble. It's obvious that without unions there would have been huge hordes of three-dollar-an-hour peons building the pipeline, just as two-fifty-an-hour peons slaved away during the drilling and exploration phase of the oil fiasco. And finally, the unions have begun to support Alaska workers.

I went down to Fairbanks' new state building one morning to see if I could wrangle a residency card. (There's a new rule for pipeline work now: no residency card, no pipeline work. Unless of course there are no qualified residents to do the work.) The line was long and full of people discussing elaborate ploys to convince the interviewers that they were residents of Alaska. Probably only one out of ten would meet all the requirements. A man of about fifty-five pushed his way to the front of the line. "I've been living in this state for nineteen years now," he shouted at the interviewer. "I don't see why I need any goddamn residency card, and I damn sure don't see why I need to stand in your fucking line!" That was the right approach. Only an Alaskan would act that way. He was processed quickly.

On the other hand I knew an old truck driver who had spent the last twenty years migrating from Fairbanks to Acapulco and back again, working six months in Alaska and spending six months on the beach. He was righteously pissed off about this new bureaucratic interference in his lifestyle. That should count in his favor. You're at least an honorary Alaskan when you start to think about killing bureaucrats.

One of the most popular fantasies of that species known as the Fairbanks hippie concerns selling out, going south, and buying a farm. A mutual friend of ours sold her log cabin and two acres, and for the same price bought forty acres and a house in Oregon. It seemed like a good trade. One of the main reasons that so many young anarchists came to Alaska in the first place was so that they could get their hands on some land. Once upon a time, Alaskan dirt was free for the taking, but now any old piece of worthless swamp is worth at least a couple thousand dollars an acre! The close of the homesteading days also marked the end of the old fashioned Alaskan dream of self-sufficiency, living off the land and with the land. That is no more. The business of Alaska, as in the rest of the United States, is business. But maybe, in a way having something perhaps to do with karma and poetic justice, the Alaskan back-to-the-landers have finally gotten what they wanted. When the business of Alaska became business rather than staying alive, those little chunks of dirt that poor people bought for a hundred dollars down and seventy-five dollars a month became very valuable. Maybe, after all, it worked out. Those who came north in the late sixties and early seventies with enough money to buy land that was free now have the money to buy land that costs five or six hundred an acre—American farm land.

I happened to notice again the stack of papers that Elaine had saved for me so I could do my research on the pipeline. I had been in Fairbanks a week now, and hadn't looked at them.

My interest in the pipeline was flagging. As slowly as ever, as inefficiently as ever, the line is nearing completion. Once a week Alyeska issues a statement saying that the pipeline is 55.9 percent complete or 62.5 percent complete, and the newspapers dutifully print the figure. It's all business as usual, so far as they are concerned. On the other hand, the media has taken to describing the amount of pipe that needs to be torn up and rewelded, or at least re-X-rayed, in miles. The first linear report that I heard was fifty miles, or 8.25 percent of the line. The latest claimed that 200 miles, or 25 percent of the pipeline, was of questionable integrity. Alyeska has suggested that it could be extremely damaging to the environment to dig up two hundred miles of pipe and X-ray the welds. They are aiming at their favorite solution to problems of quality: lower the standards. It is not common pipeline practice to X-ray every weld, and now that two hundred miles of pipe is held together by uncertified welds, Alyeska suggests that the problem with the Alaska Pipeline is that the requirements are too stringent. Problem solving by legislation: it's a familiar shuck.

At the same time, Jerry Ford has appointed a commission to go to Alaska and find out just what the problem is. It is impossible to predict the outcome of such a move. Government commissions are notorious for seeing what they want to see, and there is a great deal of pressure on them to discover that everything is just fine. What's good for Alyeska is good for America, no question about that. Jerry Ford, however, once assured the American public that the pipeline would meet the stiff requirements that were set for it. But then he's no longer around.

The day may be saved, however, by a "technological breakthrough," the mysterious process of acoustical holography. The complexities of acoustical holography are so far beyond me that I will make no attempt to suggest that it will work or not work. The process seems to involve bouncing sound waves off the pipe—from the inside—and somehow catching the waves on the rebound so as to form a three-dimensional picture of each of the welds. I'm excited about acoustical holography, though it is suspicious that this technological breakthrough occurred just in the nick of time to save Alyeska from having to disinter two hundred miles of their pipeline.

Meanwhile, I had met this woman, who knew this guy, who knew another guy, who almost definitely knew how many people had gotten killed while building the pipeline. "I'll find out," she said. "You just leave it to me." That seemed to be the only thing I had left to find out. Every night Michael and I went to some bar or other where I ran into someone I had worked with in the past, and I asked them about the pipeline. "About the same," they all told me. "Same old bullshit, except that sometimes you have to pretend you're doing something instead of sleeping in the bus when there's nothing to do.'' One night I even ran into Bearclaw, my giant mountain man friend.

"Don't bother to believe all this stuff about Alyeska tightening up and trying for more production," he said. "I've been working with the same outfit for three months now, and let me tell you, we are a hell of a crew. The laborers run the show, which means we are probably the most intelligent crew on the whole fucking line. We can do the work of three crews and still take long lunch breaks. But they don't want production. Sometimes we have to *demand* that they let us work. We usually end up working about three hours a day, keep everything on an even keel.''

He rambled on excitedly about the equipment he was working with. Bearclaw hates the pipeline as much as anyone; he's a mountain man. But there is something intensely fascinating about these pieces of equipment that can do in one hour the work of a hundred men, and also in one day can tear up more country than a man with an axe and shovel would in a lifetime. We drove around town, enthusiastically calling out to each other, "Look, there's a new D-9 with a ripper!" and "Wow! A hammerhead crane—the first in Fairbanks!" There is something about sidling up next to a piece of equipment that cost so much and can destroy so much. Equipment grows on you. I never thought that I would find myself stopping beside the freeway in northern California to talk to a crew that was building a pipeline. Small pipe, you understand. They were using cranes to set it into the ditch instead of sideboom Caterpillars. "Now, up on the Alaska Pipeline . . .'' I told these boys.

I had come to Fairbanks with no definite plans about how long I might be there. But in the middle of the second week I knew that I wasn't going to last very long. It was the old "woman problem," something I remembered all too well. Sheer, total, uncontrollable horniness. The "woman problem" seemed to be the one thing about Fairbanks that hadn't changed in the least. There are very few unattached

women in the north—the ones you see getting off the plane
are usually on their way to join a man who has fast-talked
them into coming up for the winter. Unless of course they
happen to be lesbians, of which Fairbanks seems to have
more than its share. As Michael told me, "You see, you
gotta have balls to live in Alaska."

"Fuck the last frontier," I said. "I'm going back to
sunny California. California girls, awright!"

"Maybe I'll come with you," said Michael. "Let's
smoke another joint."

Before leaving I once again contacted the woman who
had a friend who had a friend who almost certainly knew
how many people had been killed while working on the
pipeline. "He knows," she told me, "but he's not talking. I
guess that's just a number Alyeska would rather not have
anyone know. It must be a rather large number."

"Yeah," I said. "I guess it must be."